T0077668

The Curse Causeless

By Carolyn H. Ingram

Order this book online at www.trafford.com
or email orders@trafford.com

Most Trafford titles are also available at major online book retailers.

© Copyright 2008, 2015 by Carolyn H. Ingram.
All rights reserved. No part of this publication may be reproduced, stored in a retrieval
system, or transmitted, in any form or by any means, electronic, mechanical, photocopying,
recording, or otherwise, without the written prior permission of the author.

Printed in the United States of America.

ISBN: 978-1-4251-8089-8 (sc)

Library of Congress Control Number: 2009913519

Because of the dynamic nature of the Internet, any web addresses or links contained in
this book may have changed since publication and may no longer be valid. The views
expressed in this work are solely those of the author and do not necessarily reflect the
views of the publisher, and the publisher hereby disclaims any responsibility for them.

Any people depicted in stock imagery provided by Thinkstock are models,
and such images are being used for illustrative purposes only.
Certain stock imagery © Thinkstock.

Scripture quotations marked KJV are from the Holy Bible, King James Version
(Authorized Version). First published in 1611. Quoted from the KJV Classic
Reference Bible, Copyright © 1983 by The Zondervan Corporation.

Trafford rev. 11/26/2014

www.trafford.com
North America & international
toll-free: 1 888 232 4444 (USA & Canada)
fax: 812 355 4082

Dedicated to the **Glory of God**
Through the **Lord Jesus Christ**

and to the two Lila's
in my life:

Lila Pearl Hardeman, my mother
Lila Alexis Hudson, my daughter

As the bird by wandering,
As the swallow by flying,
So the curse causeless
Shall not come . . .

Seven Days To Judgment

The First Day
(*Nightmare*)

"Do you heah me, boy?" the man cocked the trigger of his pistol and pressed the barrel against the young slave's temple.

"Yes, suh! I heah."

Tension electrified the muggy night air. The first speaker continued in his soft, deadly drawl.

"If you cross me, I'll find you and blow your brains out. Then I'll sell your wench and those brats of yours."

A flash of anger crossed the black man's face. "You ain't got no call to do dat to dem! I been servin' you faithful all this time."

"You sassing me, nigger?"

"No, suh, but I don't want mah fam'ly hurt."

"If you do exactly as you're told and keep your mouth shut about it, they won't be."

The white man holstered his gun but did not release his grip on the slave's frayed shirt collar. He then shoved him in the direction of the nearby army camp. The black man stumbled amidst the dense undergrowth, regained his balance, and ran through the woods toward his assigned destination. The white man led his horse deftly through the forest in the opposite direction. Through the foliage the moonlight glittered on the gray and gold of his uniform.

He climbed up a steep bank onto the road where others like him were gathered. Mounting his horse, he gave a signal, and they galloped westward. The horses' hooves flung back clods of earth as they sped along.

A restless sleeper tossed and turned upon her bed, in the throes of a nightmare. She wanted to wake up, but was powerless to do so.

Suddenly, a single rifle short crackled in the air like a thunderbolt.

Olivia sprang upright in her bed. Beads of sweat dotted her forehead. Her breath came in short gasps, and she trembled uncontrollably. Once again, she told herself that it was only a dream.

(In a dream, in a vision of the night, when deep sleep falleth upon men, in slumberings upon the bed: Then He openeth the ears of men, and sealeth their instruction. - Job 33:15-16)

****

The Second Day
(Missions and Motives)

Friday
June 30, 2000
7:00 a.m.

Early morning sunlight has a way of dispelling the terrors of the night. And so it was with Olivia Perry. Seated at her breakfast table, the newly retired history professor glanced at her morning paper, already unfolded as though blatantly demanding her attention to its front page. Today she would not be able to filter the lead story through her intellectual mesh of curiosity and skepticism; her heart was too close to it. She felt quite unequal to reading it at the moment. Nor was she yet prepared to grapple with the research notes for her first book.

No, she generously gave her mind the luxury of wandering. She began to reminisce about her long teaching career, one that had lasted well over a quarter of a century. Like restless moths to a candle's flame, her thoughts were drawn to a specific year and a special group of students, although, unlike the moths, she knew very well that she would be burned. However, she could not resist. The year was 1979, the place, Jackson State University in Jackson, Mississippi. Rather than attend class that morning, most of her students had chosen instead to gather with others on the Plaza as Iranian exchange students staged a demonstration ...

>   *Leader: "Down with the Shah!"*
>   *Demonstrators: "Down with the Shah!"*
>   *Leader: "Blacks are our brothers!"*
>   *Demonstrators: "Blacks are our brothers!"*
>   *Leader: "End all oppression!"*
>   *Demonstrators: "End all oppression!"*

3

*There were many cheers and much clamor. Standing
at some distance apart, Olivia was still able to discern Jude
Ramadan. Even if she had not seen him, the voice would have
been unmistakable because she had heard it so many times
debating in her Western Civilization class. He, of course, was
the leader. Jude and his comrades occupied the upper level
of the Plaza which was attained by a flight of steps. Their
audience congregated at the base of the steps on the main level.*

*Professor Perry repositioned herself so that she could
observe the faces of the listeners without being considered one
of them. She spotted two that she privately referred to as the
"dynamic duo": John Henderson and Scott Kendricks, both
starting players on the basketball team. Leaning against John
possessively was Antoinette Dixon, his latest girlfriend. Then
Olivia's gaze zoomed in on the person next to Scott, and a
frown wrinkled her brow. It was Nathan, her son..*

B-r-r-i-n-g! The shrill ringing of the telephone
interrupted her disturbing reflection.

"Mom Olivia? How are you this morning?"

"Oh, good morning, Damaris," she responded with
cautious pleasure to the voice of her daughter-in-law. I'm
quite well, thank you. And how are you and those two
men of yours?"

"We're just fine. Of course, you know that we will
pay you a long overdue visit tomorrow in spite of
everything else. You didn't forget, did you?"

Olivia gave a short, mirthless laugh. "Forget? How
could I even if I wanted to? That 'everything else,' as you
call it, made this morning's headlines."

She glanced at the front page of *The Vicksburg Post* and read aloud, "'**June 30, 2000.** *Freedom Party Presidential Contender Nathan Perry's Campaign Trail Leads to Vicksburg.*'"

The two women conversed for a few minutes more during which Olivia told her son's wife that she'd planned a small gathering on the evening of their arrival. Then Damaris said that she had to hurry and finish dressing because she and Richard were accompanying Nathan to his office. Olivia uttered a hasty good-bye and hung up the receiver. Her hand twitched slightly in nervous agitation.

**Friday
June 30, 2000
9:30 a.m.**

Several miles east of Vicksburg in Bovina, Mississippi, a minister sat in his office staring out the window which opened onto the playground of Apostles' Creed Christian Academy. His eyes stared but did not see, for his mind was otherwise occupied. He was a man of about forty with sharply cut facial features. There was a firmness about his lips and chin which hinted at purpose and strength but a wistfulness in his eyes that seemed to undermine them. The approach of middle age had somewhat thickened the waist of his six-foot, three-inch frame, yet it still showed signs of an athlete's musculature. He gazed at the verdant field beyond the chain link fence encircling the playground. *"Without a vision, the people perish,"* he contemplated.

And, yes, he did have a vision for expanding the school to include grades six, seven, and eight, those turbulent, impressionable years in students' lives. He wanted to positively impact them at this pivotal stage. The facility to accommodate the additional students would be erected on the adjacent lot once the church purchased the property. Yet, he was hesitant. *"Why?"* he asked himself.

Suddenly a shrill whistle alerted him that one of the teachers on duty needed immediate assistance. He covered the space between his desk and the door in microseconds, dashed down the corridor and was soon outside running toward the fence. Two ten-year-old boys were rolling about violently on the ground. One gripped his opponent in a headlock while the other combatant punched at him wildly, desperately trying to free himself. Making his way through the student spectators and the two female teachers exercising crowd control, Scott Kendricks reached down and grabbed a dusty fighter in each hand.

He marshalled them to his office. At first, he smiled inwardly, thinking, *"Boys will be boys,"* and felt an affinity with them. The episode had evoked memories of his own boyhood battles. Then he realized that this was the *fifth* fight in less than two weeks of the school's summer enrichment program. Was there something more than youthful high spirits operating here? He glanced backward beyond the fence at the vacant lot where poplar trees stood majestically and the emerald-colored grass bowed delicately before the hot breeze. But neither trees nor grass could answer his troubling question. On the other side of the lot westward, he could just barely discern a white sign painted with bold black letters. He did not strain to read it, for he knew all to well what it said: **Demeter**.

Since the day that Scott and the elders had first broken ground for the ministry complex, he had felt an unexplainable wariness whenever he beheld the looming tract adjacent to the land that he now wanted for expansion. Named for the Grecian goddess of agriculture and fruitfulness, the Demeter tract for several hundred feet ran parallel to the western boundary of the vacant lot then curved back upon itself. Stately pine and cedar trees marked Demeter's property line and formed the entrance to a thick woods. Like the fertile pagan deity, the land seemed poised to enfold within its ample bosom not only the lot next to it but Apostles' Creed itself. But something restrained it, and it encroached no further—for now.

The pastor walked between the boys with a hand firmly clamped on the tensed shoulder of each young warrior. The three entered the side door of the school building and strode a few feet down the hall to Scott's office. He glimpsed his reflection in the wall mirror beside his door--clergyman's collar, white short-sleeved shirt and black vest, and a face which seemed accustomed to frowning in intense deliberation.

Simultaneously, another face, hundreds of miles away, also stared at a mirror image of itself and frowned in displeasure; however, the reason had more to do with vanity rather than with contemplation. Scott knew John Henderson, the owner of the other face, quite well. He was a man whose friendship the minisister highly valued--and whose fate he greatly feared.

John checked his appearance in the ornately framed mirror, looking doubtfully at his face from which he had recently shorn a neat salt-and-pepper beard. Only the mustache remained, which he refused to sacrifice, even for the sake of public image. *"Man, I hope she can get used to this. For that matter, I hope I can!"* he thought. He had been waiting for half an hour in the outer office of his former college classmate and newest client, Congressman Nathan Sundiata Perry. Restless impatience would not allow him to sit down for more than five minutes at a time.

Just then the Congressman's private office door swung open and Nathan, his wife Damaris, and their six-year-old son Richard emerged. Since John Henderson had taken charge of Nathan's presidential campaign, he yielded only to Perry's immediate family in claiming rights to the candidate's time. As Nathan and Damaris stood in the doorway, he sensed a slight strain between the two of them, though they were smoothing it over with pleasantries and easy graciousness.

Richard, however, was oblivious to the tension between his parents and bounded toward his father's campaign manager shouting, "Hey, Uncle Johnny!"

"Hey, Rich!" returned Henderson and immediately dropped to one knee. "Put 'em up!"

The young boy immediately assumed his version of a boxer's stance and they shadow boxed briefly until John pretended to be disabled by Richard's right cross.

"Now, that's enough, Richard. You'll kill Uncle John before he helps your father to become President," quipped Damaris, stepping between them. "Then what will our country do?"

John's eyes met hers quickly in reaction to the possible hint of sarcasm but found her gaze inscrutable. From their formal introduction several years ago until now, John had distrusted and disliked Damaris. The fact that her father was Jewish did little to increase her appeal. *"How could any self-respecting black woman allow herself to be considered a Jew?"* he had thought upon their initial meeting and had not since changed his opinion.

He replied cheerily, "There's no chance of that. In January the White House will be enlivened with some *much needed* color." His emphasis and meaning were both very clear.

"We won't get anywhere near it if you openly make remarks like that," warned Nathan disapprovingly. "Remember, 'All voting ballots are red, white, and blue.' Isn't that our latest official campaign slogan for those who want to bring in the race issue?" His sarcasm, unlike his wife's, was unmistakable.

"Touche," conceded John, checked but not capitulating.

"Come on, sweetheart," Damaris put her arm around Richard's shoulder and steered him toward the outer door. "Daddy and Uncle John have to discuss political business."

Richard was dutifully exiting with his mother, but he couldn't resist turning and making an announcement to John. "Uncle Johnny, guess what? My dad's birthday is next week. Let's you and me give him a party! Just us guys." He smiled at his mother consolingly. "How about it?"

"Man, you know, that's a good idea," responded John, feigning surprise at this revelation. "Let me get back to you on that. Okay, Rich?" He glanced questioningly at Richard's father who shook his head almost imperceptibly.

"Promise?" urged Richard as his mother ushered him out the door.

"I promise."

After the door closed behind them, John resumed their conversation. "When I first took on your campaign, didn't I tell *you* that the image makes the reality possible? Once the public is captivated by a man's image, they are so enthralled by *it* that they do not, no, they _cannot_ see *him*. So, he gives the people what *they* want; then, he can do what *he* wants. Be assured, Nathan, I haven't forgotten your ultimate objective; it has also been mine for the past two decades. That ballot slogan is simply part of the image that will help you to accomplish that objective. You will agree that I am a capable image maker?"

Nathan thought of John's track record. He headed one of the most controversial yet sought-after public relations firms in Washington, D. C. He was a "spin" virtuoso who could have gotten the grand dragon of the Ku Klux Klan appointed as director of the National Association for the Advancement of Colored People (NAACP).

"If you weren't the best you wouldn't be here, John, regardless of our long acquaintance and friendship. I do commend you on how you've handled the campaign thus far. And as for my 'ultimate objective,' we'll deal with that later. Right now, I want to win this election like I want to take my next breath."

"Then breathe easily, Congressman, for you *will* win. We agree that I excel at what I do. Make sure to remember that when you're inaugurated *and* when you receive my final bill," returned John.

He now sought to lighten the atmosphere before presenting his Mississippi strategy.

"Actually, I deserve a bonus for personal sacrifice," he stroked his chin ruefully. "I shaved my beard so that your campaign manager could project a 'clean-cut' look to your public in the Deep South."

Nathan could feel his annoyance dissipating in spite of himself. By this time they were seated in his private office. "So, when are we scheduled to take on Vicksburg?"

"Our e.t.a. is high noon on **Saturday, July 1,** where the mayor will officially welcome you at a reception at City Hall. After a tour of the Vicksburg National Military Park, you'll check in at the Linden Plantation Bed and Breakfast, where you'll stay for the duration of your visit. Promptly at 11:00 a.m. on **Sunday, July 2,** you'll address the congregation at Bethel African Methodist Episcopal Church. **Monday, July 3,** will find you paying a courtesy call on the Freedom Party's U. S. congresswoman, your former opponent. Her home is in the area, and she is on vacation from Washington. Of course the highlight of your Vicksburg trip will be your **Fourth of July** speech delivered on the grounds of the Old Court House Museum. **Wednesday, July 5,** brings you to Jackson for a meeting with the Party's legislators at the Capitol with a press conference immediately following. Then it's off to Jackson International Airport for the flight back to D. C."

Nathan removed his glasses, cleaned the lenses, and returned them to his face, a gesture which he habitually made before becoming confrontational. "Now, tell me *why* each of these events has a place on my itinerary because I know that you have a specific reason for each one."

"As we know, Congressman Perry, one must *always* have a reason for every political move that one makes. I'll gladly detail each one of mine: **(1)** The Linden Plantation was established in 1827 by John Wesley Vick, the son of Vicksburg's founder. Your staying there shows your respect for the heritage of the Old South, even though your forefathers were slaves in it. **(2)** Bethel A. M. E. Church was the first black church established in Mississippi. Making it the scene of your first formal speech of this visit shows reverence for God and for your ethnic roots.

(3) The Independence Day speech staged at the museum has enormous significance. There would *be* no Old Court House Museum were it not for the skilled slave laborers who constructed the building in 1858. An unsurrendered Confederate flag is displayed within its walls, and a victorious Union flag was raised from its cupola on July 4,1863, when the city fell to Ulysses S. Grant. It has been the scene of speeches by Jefferson Davis, the slaveholding president of the Confederacy, and by Booker T. Washington, the ex-slave who became a famed educator and the president of Tuskegee Institute. Exhibits housed in the museum reflect the multicultural heritage of the area dating back to pre-historic Native American artifacts. What better site to promote your platform of national strength in a diversified union?

"Finally, no matter what antagonisms were spawned during the primaries, *you,* won the Freedom Party's presidential nomination. It is now to *your* advantage to advocate party solidarity. Thus, we see the need of meeting with your party's representatives at the state and national levels. And, of course, we must begin narrowing the field of choice for your running mate."

Nathan paused for a moment, then spoke, "I like the sound of all that. The itinerary has my approval, but I do want to add something—a visit with my mother."

John hesitated for a split second and said, "May I ask why?"

"You shouldn't have to ask why. She's my *mother.*"

"Yes, and she's my former professor whom I truly respect and admire, but she's also one of the most outspoken black activists in Mississippi. Have you forgotten her speech last year in support of paying African Americans damages for this country's centuries of slavery? She delivered it, *uninvited* and *unexpectedly,* in the rotunda of the state Capitol building during a joint session of the legislature and was almost arrested."

"So? She's not running for office; I am. Besides, she did that in reaction to a bill introduced in Congress to compensate the descendents of Japanese Americans who had been confined to internment camps in the U.S. during World War II. She never disputed their right to reparations, *but* she *did* assert that black slavery in the U.S. predated that offense and that it was the greater wrong. Therefore, the government was obligated to pay compensation for it *first.* And, John, I remember that *you* openly endorsed many of my mother's views when you were her student. You claimed that she helped to 'liberate' your mind."

"She did, and I'll always be grateful to her for that. But this is not about gratitude, Nathan; it's about expedience. Having voters link you with her and her beliefs is *not* politically expedient, and you know this."

"But, it's *your* job to make certain that *every* part of this trip serves my political interests, isn't it, John? I know that you'll say and do whatever is necessary to fix it."

(Deliver my soul, O Lord, from lying lips, and from a deceitful tongue.- Psalm 120:2)

Friday
June 30, 2000
Noon

"CYPRESS VALE Mansion Inn: The Old South Made New." The sign was engraved in stone and inset in the brick wall on either side of the wrought iron gate of the main entrance. In long-gone antebellum days, a three-story warehouse had stood on the site, property of Julius Pembroke, then one of Vickburg's foremost citizens. Fronting the warehouse site had been (and still was) a commodious dock, built to facilitate the shipping of Pembroke cotton downriver to New Orleans. His actual plantation had been located outside Bovina. Julius had committed the day-to-day running of the vast farm to his overseer, Robert Forrest, who lived on site with his wife, the former Rebecca Carlisle, and their two children. The Pembrokes had chosen to reside in the city. Wagonloads of cotton bales would arrive in Vicksburg from the plantation and make their way to the river. Like a liquid magnet, the mighty Mississippi drew the energy of the city unto itself. The waterfront bustled with commerce. Buyers representing monied Yankee interests finalized deals with the agents of local planters and sometimes with the planters themselves. Here Julius' cash crop had been unloaded from both wagons and warehouse and put aboard riverboats bound for New Orleans and from there to the textile mills of the East Coast and beyond.

On their way to the Crescent City, these vessels had steamed past a magnificent Georgian mansion poised on one of the steep bluffs overlooking the river. The wooded hills surrounding the bluff seemed to fall away to give the house preeminence. This had been the original Cypress Vale. During the pre-war days of its glory, guests of Julius Pembroke arriving by riverboat disembarked at Cypress Landing where elegant, lightweight carriages driven by liveried Negro coachmen awaited to transport them to the main house. They ascended the winding path that cut through the abundant deciduous forest sloping up from the river. The end of the elevated course revealed the mansion, resplendent against the wide sweep of the Misssissippi River making its way to the sea. It had been a scene meant to strikingly convey a sense of their host's wealth and dominance. And it had fulfilled that purpose.

Some twenty miles east, on the actual plantation, hundreds of acres of fleecy white fields were speckled with the dark forms of black men, women, and children held in bondage, bending their backs to pick the cotton that made Cypress Vale possible.

The mansion scene had been immortalized in 1856 by a painting which now hung imposingly in the foyer of the inn. As a child, Julia Pembroke had been captivated by it as she had been by the family accounts of the exploits of her great-grandfather, Julius. She had always gloried in being his namesake (to the extent that gender would allow.) Now, as a dowager of sixty years and the mistress of the inn, Julia Pembroke Leigh often gazed at the painting with pride and longing.

When she and her late husband Andrew had purchased this present property in 1990, it had been her fervent desire to re-create the splendor of her ancestral home. Granted, it would be on a physically smaller scale, but the essence of affluence, nobility, and prestige must be there. She had begun by bestowing upon the property the name of her family estate. With that gesture she had challenged herself to "make it so." The task had become her mission—no, it was more personal than that—to her it was a trust, a charge given to her by heritage and a debt owed by her to posterity. It had been her passion for the past decade.

With Andrew's demise five years ago, she had been forced to restructure her finances in order to keep Cypress Vale. At that time she had made the decision to convert the mansion to a hotel. She had determined that "the Vale" would cater to only "the right sort of people." This meant those who appreciated, if not reverenced, Southern tradition and who would relish being considered "elite" enough to pay a premium to spend a night (or two, or three, etc.) ensconced in it. Mrs. Andrew Leigh never permitted sentiment to thwart shrewd business sense. She saw no reason why the two could not complement each other quite profitably. Indeed, she had operated under this belief since she had established the inn, and both she and it had prospered admirably. Julius would have been proud of her.

Julia now steered her car through the open gate and up the long, curved driveway that was the main entrance to Cypress Vale. The beautifully maintained cypress trees bordering the pavement on either side did not evoke the feeling of calm well being and deserved self satisfaction that she usually experienced when driving onto her property. The front page news that morning galled her.

She was undecided as to why she felt threatened by the much publicized arrival of Nathan Perry in Vicksburg. True, on key political issues they were diametrically opposed. True, his votes in Congress had cost her economically. True, he was an uppity colored (she had never adopted the terms "black" or "African American" in her thought life) boy from Mississippi who was full of himself. "But what is the real danger that I see in him?" she pondered. As though in answer to the question, she blurted out, "How *dare* he?" For if this colored man dared to aspire to the Presidency—and succeeded—how much more would others of his kind dare? So, there it was. Apparently, she was not quite as racially tolerant as she had self-righteously thought.

Now she could mentally step back from her conclusion and determine her response to Nathan Perry and all that he represented.

Friday
June 30, 2000
12:30 p.m.

The drive to Bovina that afternoon was not unenjoyable for Olivia. The mainly rural landscape had a pleasing blend of rustic homesteads, small business establishments, and graceful country manors. *"Only for a former student would I interrupt my leisure time so soon after securing it,"* she thought. Often this summer she had reminded herself of this. When she first agreed to

18

teach an afternoon class in his enrichment program, she had been touched by the sincerity and earnestness of Scott Kendricks's request, not to mention its boost to her already vigorous ego. However, being obligated to teach three afternoons a week without pay was irksome at times. *"Well, at least today is Friday, and we'll be finished with the whole thing by the end of next month."*

She maneuvered her beloved and seemingly eternal Chrysler Fifth Avenue onto the parking lot of Apostles' Creed Worship Center and drove past the sanctuary to the academy buildings. Her class began right after lunch, and she liked to arrive at least a half hour early to "prepare the atmosphere for learning." Olivia knew that, in spite of the intrusion upon her summer, she loved teaching these children. But they did present a challenge. A post lunch class must be stimulating and engaging because the teacher is competing with the hyped aftermath of students socializing over their meal and with the contented drowsiness induced by full stomachs. By the time that the bell rang signaling her class's imminent arrival, she was ready for them. Yet, as they noisily took their seats, she soon sensed that her animated group of fifth graders were already abuzz with something other than the attention-getting word that she had scrawled across the dry erase board.

"O-o-o-h, Miz Perry, Miz Perry! Eric and Seth got into a fight on the playground at morning break time," announced Georgiana Stevenson triumphantly, eager to be the first with the worst news. Both boys shot killer looks in her direction from their seats at the rear of the classroom.

Olivia had privately dubbed Georgiana the up and coming "mouth of the South." In spite of her irritation at the child's talkativeness, she wanted to know why two of *her* students would resort to violent behavior. However, for now, she would deny the talebearer the shock effect that she sought.

Calmly she responded, "Good afternoon, Georgiana. How are you today?"

"Fine," came the puzzled reply, "did you hear what I said?"

"Of course. How could I have missed such a loud announcement? But now it's time for class, isn't it?"

Before Georgiana could reply, Olivia moved front and center to the board and spoke in the authoritative yet inviting voice to which the children had become accustomed.

"Good afternoon, class. I know that you're all having a wonderful day, and now it is about to become even better. Today in our African American Heritage class we are going to discuss [at this point she tapped the board with her pointer beneath a large word written in red] 'Cursing.'"

The children's eyes grew wide in disbelief. Had Mrs. Perry lost her mind?

"But Miz Perry," cried Georgiana, horrified, "we aren't supposed to curse, especially not at a church school. Jesus will be so mad!"

"And He very well should be, if we were going to be using profanity or 'bad words,' but I'm sure that He'll be glad that we are discussing this type of cursing because He has said that He wants us to know the truth in all things. You see, class, this kind of cursing means asking God to bring evil or harm upon someone."

"Really?" gasped Georgiana, fascinated. "Can I really do that?" her mind raced with possibilities as she thought of her bossy older sister and other annoying people in her life whom she could sincerely ask God to instantly slaughter or at least to severely maim.

"Just listen, children," Olivia continued. "Now, this story is about three brothers. Their names were Shem, Ham, and Japheth, and they lived many, many, years ago in what we now call the Middle East. These three brothers were very special because they were the only brothers left in the whole world. They had the same mother and father, but each one was a different color. God had become angry with all the evil people in the world, and He had destroyed them all with a great flood. The only people left were the three brothers, their parents, and their wives because God had shown them how to build a special boat. God also had told them to bring a male and a female of each type of animal on the boat to save them from the flood.

"Now, with the earth washed clean, God planned to start everything over. He planned to make new people from the three brothers and their wives. He also planned to divide the new world among the three brothers, giving each his own part to rule. Shem, the brown son, would get the land now known as Asia; Ham, the black son, would get the land now known as

Africa; and Japheth, the white son, would get the land now known as Europe [As Olivia spoke, she pointed to each continent on a world map suspended from hooks at the top of the dry erase board]. From these areas, God intended the new people to branch out into the rest of the world.

"But something happened. One of the brothers got into trouble before they received their special territories. One day their father was passed out drunk and lay naked in his tent. Ham saw him, but instead of covering him up and keeping quiet about it, he made fun of him and went and told his other two brothers about him. Shem and Japheth, however, did not ridicule their father but covered him up without looking at his nakedness. When their father, Noah, woke up, he realized what Ham had done and was very angry with him."

"Hey!" exclaimed Eric. This is the Noah's Ark story, from the Bible isn't it? My granny told me about that, but you tell it different. I mean, she didn't tell me much about the three brothers."

"How very smart of you to make the connection, Eric," commended Olivia. "Now, let me continue. By this time Ham and his wife had already had a son. Because Noah was mad about what his son, Ham, had done to him, he cursed Ham's son, Canaan. He wanted God to make Canaan and his future descendants servants to Shem and Japheth and their descendants.

"Mrs. Perry," queried Seth earnestly, "is this the 'curse of blackness' that I've heard so much about?"

"Well, Seth, let's examine it, shall we? The Bible never states that God agreed to do what Noah said. The Bible *does* say that Ham had three other sons, and their names were Cush, Mizraim, and Phut. It also says that *all* of Ham's sons and their descendants started many great civilizations. One of them was Egypt. The Bible calls Egypt 'the land of Ham' because it was first established and settled by one of Ham's descendants. Have you ever heard of Egypt and the ancient Egyptians?"

"Oh, I know something about them!" Georgiana exclaimed. "Those were the people who built those big triangle thingies on the beach," she added smugly.

"Girl, those were the **pyramids**," corrected Seth impatiently, "and they built them in the **desert**. You're so ignorant that I can't stand it! Be quiet so we can hear the rest of the story."

Georgiana's eyes blazed, but before she could verbally return fire, Olivia resumed.

"That will be enough, you two. As I was saying, God blessed Ham's sons and their descendants with the intelligence and industry to excel in building, inventing, and exploring. They even built a tower that almost reached to heaven. Isn't that amazing?"

"Where are all of those people now?" asked Eric.

"They are seated in this classroom. They are ... *you*," Olivia said with a smile. She let them think about that a few moments.

"Now, let's focus especially on Ham and Canaan. Ham disrespected his father and made fun of his father's weakness. These attitudes of disrespect and ridicule he passed on to Canaan. To answer Seth's question, then, we must quickly review what I've told you: Ham was born black, and God was ready to give him a special part of the earth to rule, just the same as his two brothers. So, his blackness wasn't the problem. Also, Canaan and the rest of Ham's sons were born black, but Canaan took on his father's bad attitudes. His brothers did not. Again, blackness was not the problem; it *was* not and *is* not a curse. All colors of the human race are beautiful because God created them, and He considers them to be so. Skin color does not bring a curse; actions do. Ham cursed his own son by his behavior, and Canaan accepted the cursing by behaving as his father had."

"Well, it wasn't Ham's fault that his daddy got drunk and took off his clothes," declared Georgiana. "That was Noah's own fault." The rest of the class voiced their agreement. "Drunk folks do stuff like that," she continued sagely. "Ya'll shoulda seen that drunk man out in front of Chenelle's Cabaret las' night! He pulled down his pants and--

"*Thank you*, Georgiana," Olivia neatly cut her off and flashed one of her fake smiles. "Please hold that thought and share it with us later." She resumed her discourse. "Yes, it's true that Noah's drunkenness was his own fault," she conceded. "But it was *Ham's* fault that he reacted to his father's condition in the way that he did. You see class, a person who ridicules another sometimes does it because he doesn't feel too good about himself. Often he sees something in the other person

24

that reminds him of what he dislikes about himself. So, when Ham dishonored his father like that, he was really dishonoring himself."

"I'm gonna remember that the next time anybody tries to put me down," asserted Seth with a quick glance at Eric.

The look did not escape Olivia's notice, but she bided her time.

"But guess what?" continued Olivia. "Even though Ham passed on his self-dislike and self- destructiveness to Canaan, as time passed, many of Canaan's descendants changed their attitudes and behavior for the better. Jesus even chose one of them to be among His first twelve disciples. His name was Simon Zelotes, and he became an apostle, one of the special men that Jesus sent out to spread His teachings and to establish His Church throughout the world. Does Simon seem cursed by God to you?" The students unanimously responded in the negative.

Afterward there was a lively class discussion about thoughts and actions that could bring blessings rather than curses. All too soon the bell rang signaling the end of the class period and the end of the school day, which was shortened in the summer program. Olivia knew that because of the nearness of their residences to Apostles' Creed, Eric and Seth walked home. Therefore, they would not risk missing the bus by remaining a few minutes after school. As the students filed out, she asked them to stay behind.

"What's this I hear about you two fighting?"

"Mrs. Perry," began Eric, alarmed over the possibility of further punishment, "Pastor Kendricks already suspended us from school for Monday. He talked to us *and* paddled us after we told him what happened."

"Fine. Now tell *me* what happened."

Seth spoke up, "Me and Eric was—oops, sorry—*Eric* and *I* were playing dodge ball with some of the other boys at break. I was one of the ones throwing, and Eric said that I hit him too hard on purpose."

Eric did not dispute Seth's account, so Olivia gave him leave to continue.

"He got in my face and called me a name that made me mad."

Olivia looked inquiringly at Eric, who seemed decidedly uncomfortable. "What did you call him?"

Eric heaved a sigh and said, "Niggah."

Because of her reflections earlier that day, Olivia's mind flashed back more than two decades to another class in which this same topic had been discussed, but the students had been young men and women. Inwardly, she smiled, ready to pounce like a tigress on this present teachable moment. Outwardly, she managed to maintain the stern demeanor that her students' misbehavior had warranted.

"Boys," she started slowly, "let me explain something to you . . ."

(And ye shall know the truth, and the truth shall make you free. – John 8:32)

Friday
June 30, 2000
11:00 p.m.

"If he exasperates you so often, then fire him, Nathan," advised Damaris as she sat before the mirror of her dressing table gently combing through her hair.

"I would be insane to cut loose a top PR man at this stage," returned Nathan shortly. "Also, he's highly competent in handling our campaign security. You know that, Damaris."

"What I know is that he's a racist, and *you* know it as well. And tell me this, Nathan," she said, turning to face him, "Have you wondered *how* John knows the things he does about weapons, security risks, etc.? I believe that he's involved with something much more cutthroat than public relations, though he can be lethal enough even in that."

"Damaris, sweetheart, it must be marvelous for you and Moses to sit on high labeling people and handing down judgment as you do," he replied, attempting to mollify his reproof and his jibe at Judaism with a forced

27

smile. He really was not in the mood to fight about John or anything else tonight.

Richard had been duly tucked in for the evening, and his parents were having one of the campaign "discussions" that had become a common occurrence since Nathan had entered the presidential race.

"Joking about it won't solve the problem," returned Damaris tersely. Her husband had ignited her anger with his flippant remark, and she was on slow burn.

"Neither will arguing. Look, we have an early flight tomorrow and a long day following it. Let's discuss this later, shall we? I'm going to sleep."

Damaris was tempted to thrash out their differences about John then and there. But she was tired. And there was something more. She looked at Nathan lying on his back, his fingers interlocked under his head as he stared thoughtfully at the ceiling. The gem stone topaz—yes, that is what his coloring resembled. Jet black were the hairs of his head, his eyebrows, and his whiskers that formed a hint of a mustache. His eyes were shaped like almonds tilted slightly upward at the outer corners. She often said, teasingly, that he was the hieroglyph of an Egyptian pharaoh come to life. His bare torso began broadly at his shoulders and narrowed down to his trim mid-section that met the waistband of his pajamas. Nathan was lean but "cut," his muscles firm and well-toned.

She desired to be seduced and thrilled by this man who seemed so distant. She wanted to be loved back into a benevolent mood before succumbing to slumber.

Damaris gracefully slid into bed beside him but found no warmth in the connubial sheets. Though he was not yet asleep, Nathan's chest rose and fell rhythmically with his steady breathing. His eyes were now closed and his thoughts—whatever they were—puckered his brow in a slight frown.

"I don't know about the rest of Vicksburg, but my mother will be glad to see us."

"Will she really?" thought Damaris, remembering Olivia's reaction to the headlines heralding Nathan's arrival. But she left the question unspoken. She turned from him, with a muffled sigh and simply said, "Good night."

**Friday
June 30, 2000
11:45 p.m.**

Several miles up the Potomac River in northwest Washington's Georgetown, Mr. and Mrs. John Henderson were finishing a late supper. Queen Anne style furnishings were the penchant of the lady of the house, as was evident in the mahogany dining room suite with its vermillion upholstery. The cream-colored walls were accented with a rose-tinged glow emanating from the sconces. Fleurons of scarlet and gold had been painstakingly stenciled onto the walls at carefully spaced intervals. Tonight the dining room exuded passion and elegance, perfectly in accordance with the plan of Mrs. Henderson. She was well aware of the stress exerted upon her husband by these campaign trips, and she, of course, knew how to relieve it. She was determined that he would board the plane to Mississippi a happy and "rejuvenated" man.

Antoinette had given Concepcion, their diligent housekeeper, the night off. Earlier in the week, she had subtlely suggested to her twin son and daughter that a show of dedication to their studies would go far in persuading their father to finance their much-desired trip to Cairo next month. Therefore, Meji had solemnly announced to their parents that he and his sister would spend this entire weekend on the Howard University campus "to catch up on our work since we're in summer school to get ahead." The elder twin had spoken the words like a martyr, hoping that in the very near future John would be moved to reward this sacrifice with two first class plane tickets and ample vacation cash.

She basked in glowing self-satisfaction at her ability to orchestrate circumstances to her liking.

Now, the two of them relaxed in silk dressing gowns. They had finally finished the main course of their supper, having lingered over it indulgently as each fed the other, a practice they often engaged in when dining alone. A subtle, sexual excitement built from sliding the gleaming silverware delicately between a lover's waiting lips. Of this Mrs. Henderson was well aware.

John stroked his clean-shaven chin. "So you really don't mind that the beard's gone, baby?" he asked doubtfully.

"We-l-l," Antoinette began playfully, "I must admit that I'll miss its soft, warm caress against my face when I kiss you."

30

He reached across the table and caught her hand. "I have several other body members that can softly and warmly caress you, and they ache for you right now," he said enticingly.

Antoinette slid her hand deftly from his grasp and began to clear the china and silverware from the burnished wood of the dining table. John easily encircled her waist with his arm and pulled her onto his lap.

She laughingly pretended to protest, "John! Wait. There's key lime pie for dessert."

"What I want is sweeter than any pie," he whispered. His mouth found hers, and his kiss was hungry and demanding. Her lips responded in kind and dared him to go further. Soon he was on his feet with Antoinette's supple, yielding body throbbing in his arms. The whole house was solely theirs tonight, and he relished the thought of making love to his wife wherever he chose.

Gently, he laid her on the luxuriant, shaggy fibers of the sable rug in the living room. Her loosened dressing gown fell away in the process. She stretched out her body seductively ready to receive him.

And then the telephone in the foyer loudly rang.

John knew that he could not ignore a late night phone call on the eve of a campaign trip; something may have arisen to upset his well-laid plans. He pressed his lips and tongue against the warm flesh of Antoinette's neck as an erotic downpayment on the ectasy yet to come. Then he got quickly to his feet and hurried away in the direction of the incessant ringing. He vehemently wrenched the receiver from its cradle, ready to dispatch the interruption in seconds.

"Hello!" he shouted.

"Asalamalakim, my brother." The full, resonant voice still carried a trace of its Iranian accent. It was Jude Ramadan.

****

The Third Day
(Plots, Plans, and
Discovery)

Saturday
July 1, 2000
After Midnight

The fluorescent numbers on the clock radio were luminous in the darkness. Julia turned restlessly on the silk sheets. Her gaze fell upon the nightstand; "12:15 a.m." the clock read.

"A new day," she thought fleetingly. But it was the events of the previous one which now stole her sleep. They replayed in her mind ceaselessly. Most stubborn was the conversation that had transpired in the room directly below her second-floor bedroom:

She and her special guest were in the center room of the main floor. Known as the Master's Drawing Room, it was ambitiously modeled after the study of Julius Pembroke in the original Cypress Vale mansion. It was entered from the central hallway through dark walnut double doors, the handles of which formed the initials C V when they came together. They opened directly across from the fireplace where Carlisle Forrest now stood.

Flanking the fireplace on each side was a floor-to-ceiling window with a magnificent view of the Mississippi River. On the left-hand side of the room, midway between the window and the double doors, sat an empire style desk. On the right-hand side across from the desk stood a high-backed sofa with royal blue upholstery on which Julia sat. The center back of the sofa and its oval "wings" were all edged with ornately carved wood, the graceful curves of which were repeated in the cabriole legs. Matching chairs complemented the sofa and were placed accommodatingly about the room. Built-in book shelves covered each wall except the one containing the windows. Over-looking the scene in undisputed preeminence, a full-length portrait of Julius Pembroke hung over the fireplace.

The hostess prided herself on the regal decor of the room, but the topic of conversation threatened to mar her pleasure.

"What do you think of him, Carlisle?"

"My dear Mrs. Leigh, Congressman Nathan Perry is not a person on whom I waste much thought," he lied. A frown briefly creased the forehead framed by wavy white hair.

"Perhaps it's time that you did," returned Julia shortly.

"Are you concerned about anything in particular?"

She was in no mood to play verbal cat-and-mouse games with him.

"Whatever concerns Cypress Vale and my money concerns me intensely. If Perry gets the chance to enact his plans for so called 'immigration reform,' he will decimate my hotel staff and ultimately send my operating costs soaring."

"Madam, do you _really_ believe that Perry will gain the Presidency?" his voice lilted with contempt at the thought.

"Well, I didn't believe that he would win the Freedom Party's nomination either, but that didn't stop him from doing so, did it?"

Carlisle leaned a bent elbow against the sturdy hickory mantelpiece, admiring the polished luster of the wood. His forehead rested against his hand as he starred thoughtfully into the empty fireplace.

"<u>That</u> wasn't supposed to happen," he stated quietly, more to himself than to Julia. The underlying anger in his voice suggested that he referred to more than just the unpredictability of fate.

"What do you mean?" she asked, puzzled.

He looked at her with an enigmatic smile but said nothing.

"Carlisle."

"Yes, Julia?" His use of her first name cued her that he might be willing to speak more frankly.

"How will having Perry as president affect Demeter and the new project that the Commission is planning?

"If his voting record in the House is any indication, he could seriously hinder us with land use regulations, among other things. The Demeter Complex is near completion. That's over 1300 acres which investors have prepared with roads, water, electrical power, and sewer facilities. Furthermore, I've been authorized to acquire the two properties bordering the development on the east if we need more land. I don't foresee any problem persuading the ministry that owns one of the lots to sell; most of these preachers secretly worship the 'almighty' dollar. We've erected model buildings easily adaptable to both manufacturing and industrial research and development. The site's nearness to Vicksburg and the Port place it in a Foreign Trade Zone, a fact that renders it all the more attractive to prospective international tenants. There's much to be lost if Perry blocks our progress."

Here he digressed briefly. "I shall always be grateful for your father's foresight in selling the remaining acres of the family's former plantation to the Commission back in '86. Even then I sensed your persuasive influence in his decision." He joined her on the sofa. "Therefore," he spoke softly, taking her hand and pressing it to his lips in a gentle kiss, "I am forever grateful to <u>you,</u> dear Julia."

He continued in his former more business-like manner. "I have invested heavily in developing and marketing Demeter and have enticed several manufacturers to locate plants there. They are truly enamored of her. She has the potential to garner millions for my associates and me."

Julia had come to be alternately amused and offended at Carlisle's ability to describe any given business deal as a woman that he was either seducing or pimping.

"I am also looking to get in on the upcoming development deal on the river. The Commission is already courting potential investors for it."

"And you really believe that Nathan Perry can stop all of this?"

"Didn't he defy hell and high water in Congress to deprive you and your fellow hoteliers of your precious wetbacks?" returned Carlisle hotly. His response reminded her of his volatile temper. His use of the ethnic slur bespoke his tendency for viciousness against opposition. "You can kiss <u>that</u> cheap labor gold mine good-bye."

Julia was silent as she remembered what high hopes she and other members of the American Hoteliers and Innkeepers Association had harbored for immigration legislation that would ensure a constant flow of workers to solve hotel staffing problems. In the United States House of Representatives, Nathan Perry had given a rousing speech indicting corporations for "selling out American workers while simultaneously exploiting foreign nationals." Needless to say, the bill had not passed. She sighed resignedly, poising herself to ask the next question.

"Does the Commission plan to do anything about him?" she ventured cautiously.

"We do."

He could feel her unspoken question in the air. He cupped his ex-lover's chin in his hand and looked directly into her eyes, "In the words of the immortal Shakespeare's Macbeth, 'Be innocent of the knowledge, dearest chuck, till thou applaud the deed.'"

Julia flung herself onto her back and starred intently at the darkened ceiling as though straining to discover some solace hidden there. Tiny beads of sweat accumulated at the point where her brows had knitted themselves together. But the darkness withheld both slumber and peace.

(Thus my heart was grieved, and I was pricked in my conscience. – Psalm 73:21)

Saturday
July 1, 2000
After Midnight

The *Scheherazade* Casino was an opulent place of incongruities. Externally it was an actual riverboat with a gigantic paddle wheel and two magnificent funnels, the tops of which were carved into the shapes of jeweled turbans. Internally it was fashioned like the dwelling of a sultan—or at least like the Western stereotype of one.

Some of the gaming tables were attended by scantily clad young women reminiscent of belly dancers. Their exotic allure belied their shrewdness in assuring the house's advantage at each turn of a card or twirl of a wheel. Other tables were controlled by young men garbed in white linen shirts with vests and trousers of matching dark or muted hues. Splashes of bright color appeared briefly as sashes around their waists. Dark skullcaps finely trimmed in the colors of the sashes covered their heads. The carpeting resembled a Persian rug; special lighting enhanced the gorgeous jewel-tone colors woven into intricate arabesque patterns at regular intervals. The different gambling areas were entered through portals shaped like minarets. Music, subtle but potent and exciting, infused the atmosphere.

And then there was the casino owner. Dressed conservatively but always tastefully, he moved discreetly among his patrons. His aspect was that of reserved politeness and courtesy. The discerning observer, however, would not miss Jude's veiled look of disdain, though all that his eyes beheld was his own. Tonight, however, he was not taking his customary stroll to review the premises. He was conversing on the phone in his private office positioned above the casino floor. The party on the other end of the line had been caught off guard at the sound of Jude's voice, but responded equably enough in spite of the surprise.

"Peace be unto you, also, Jude."

Neither man bothered to pretend that he had not kept tabs on the other since their last encounter. And both took pains not to refer to that encounter, though, indeed, it had been a collaboration in which the Central

Intelligence Agency would have been extremely interested.

"You have been well and are doing well, John. I am glad about that."

"Thank you. I'm happy that I can say the same for you."

"Indeed, Allah is most generous to his true sons. We are living proof of that, are we not? But why have we not talked sooner, my brother?" ventured Jude.

"Do real brothers need words to remain close?" parried John. "Their hearts speak out across the distances though their lips, for the sake of prudence and expedience, keep silent."

On his end of the phone line, Jude smiled, remembering how in college the two of them used to duel verbally. Often such sparring had ended in a dead heat, which had only served to increase their mutual respect—and wariness. Back then there had been a fundamental difference between the two men: Jude held a belief in "holy war" for which he was willing to die; John had a desire for black supremacy for which he determinedly lived. The "American Dream" with its enticing materialism had somewhat altered the two men in the intervening years—or so it appeared.

"Why are you calling me now, Jude? Is there something wrong?"

"You are coming to the fair city of Vicksburg, Mississippi, my home base, for the present. As your old friend, I wanted to welcome you personally in advance."

"Is that *all* that you wanted?"

"No. I wanted to know where you now stand." Jude was calculatingly blunt.

"On what?"

"On what you believe."

There was a brief yet intense pause.

"Some beliefs change; others never will." John's reply was cautious.

"Islam does not change, nor does the Nation of Islam. We were once both ardent disciples, I of the former and you of the latter. True?"

"True enough."

"Another truth is that our oppressors have not changed. Zionists and White Anglo-Saxon Protestants are alive and well as are their societal systems. Yet your candidate, our former college associate, continues to speak out that those in America are 'one nation under God.' Well, *my* God does not tolerate the kind of racial persecution and discrimination that has been perpetrated in these 'United States.'"

"Where are you going with this, Jude?" It was John's turn for bluntness.

"*Going?* Well, of course, brother, only Allah Himself knows where any one of us is *going*. Our final destination lies in His hands." He chose to be quite literal and, therefore, evasive in his response, then: "Remember that the blood of Hagar and Ishmael runs through both our veins, John."

"I am well aware of my heritage."

"Be equally aware of your obligation to it. You have the opportunity to place Nathan Perry in a position of great power, right in the faces of those who would rather die than see him there."

"What about *you*? Do *you* want him there?"

"That remains to be seen. Asalamalakim. I happily anticipate your arrival."

(Gather not my soul with sinners, nor my life with bloody men. – Psalm 26:9)

**Saturday
July 1, 2000
7:00 a.m.**

It was a busy, distracting morning for Olivia. She had manually disconnected all of the telephones in her house and had shut off her cellular phone. As the mother

40

of the Freedom Party's presidential candidate, she
had already had her fill of probing reporters, but with
Nathan's impending arrival in Vicksburg today, they
took on demon-like persistence. To worsen her unrest
and frustration, the nagging conviction that she should
review her book notes just would not cease. Finally, she
sat down resolutely at her dining room table amidst
stacks of carefully arranged file folders, telling herself,
*"Maybe I can get a little of this done before 'The Sound and the
Fury'* [her name for Nathan's campaign entourage] get
here." She opened one of the folders and was face-to-face
with a genealogy chart of her late husband's family.

Asterisks appeared beside certain names, one of
which was *Cassia Marie*. "You were a very remarkable
lady," she mused aloud. "Cassie Mae," as the Perrys
called her, had always fascinated Olivia. She had been
the first free member of the Perry family in the United
States and had given the family its name. Disdaining
to keep the last name of her former master, Cassie had
taken her husband's first name as her surname and had
bestowed it upon their three children. Shortly after her
emancipation, she had acquired several acres of land, a
miraculous feat for a black woman fresh from bondage.
Thus began a legacy of land ownership in Warren
County for the Perry family.

"But what price have we paid for this 'landed' prosperity?"
Olivia could not prevent the thought, and she quickly
chided herself for it. "Now, now, Dr. Perry, let's not
forsake reason for superstition." Still, she could not
dismiss a fact that her research thus far had revealed:
The deaths of the Perry male heirs had all occurred
seven years after they had received their real estate
inheritance. According to Olivia's mother-in-law, Helen
Love Perry, Cassie had told her only son, George, that he

would receive his land when he was thirty-three. Helen maintained that her rationale was that he would have sown his wild oats by then, and hopefully, would have married a "decent, church-going" woman and would be ready to settle down. Cassie had further required that her son be gainfully employed—either in working the land or in some other respectable occupation—several years prior to taking ownership of his property.

"She wasn't going to give all those acres to a fool or a bum, and she wanted to make sure that he was neither," Helen had quipped approvingly.

George had met his mother's stipulations and was prospering, but died of heat stroke on the eve of his fortieth birthday. His son, Will, Helen's husband had also met a premature demise. Olivia winced inwardly when she remembered Ellis Perry's sudden heart attack that had left her a widow with a sixteen-year-old son to raise. Now that son was contending for the Presidency of the United States, the country in which his father had died trying to establish true "liberty and justice for all." *"And he will turn forty within the next three days."* Olivia suddenly pressed the tips of her fingers hard against her temples, trying to compress the rising fear from her mind.

As though calling her back to the world of rational thought, the doorbell rang. She was an habitually early riser and was already dressed. Yet, she hesitated in going to the door, annoyed at the thought that it might be a reporter. Peering through one of the glass panels on either side of the front door, Olivia saw Scott Kendricks standing on her veranda. Surprised, she opened the door and welcomed him cordially as he offered apologies for the earliness of his visit.

Once they were comfortably settled in the living room with glasses of freshly squeezed orange juice, Scott presented his reason for coming.

"Dr. Perry, again I'm sorry for intruding so soon upon your busy day. But I have something important that I need to discuss with you."

"Oh?" Olivia leaned forward in her chair attentively. "Is it something dealing with the school? The students?"

"Yes, it is, though kind of indirectly. This may sound strange, but at the risk of offending you, I have to ask it. What's wrong with the Perry land in Bovina?

Her throat tightened. She coughed sharply, trying to dispel the acidic liquid from her windpipe. His unexpected question had caught her in mid-swallow.

"What?" she rasped. "What are you talking about? Why do you think that something is wrong with it?"

He rose from her sofa exasperatedly and ran his hand backward over his hair. He walked slowly toward the picture window, his deliberate steps measuring out his words before he spoke them.

"I don't know exactly and maybe my imagination is in overdrive, but just hear me out. Children on the playground behave...erratically when they get close to the fence bordering your property."

"Are you serious? Children's playground behavior is *always* unpredictable. That is why they *should* be properly supervised." She immediately regretted her accusatory tone, realizing that it was her defense mechanism against an unwelcome possibility.

He, however, did not appear to notice. Now he was pacing back and forth, compelled by a sense of urgency.

"Yesterday after school one of the fifth grade boys was hurrying past that section of fence on his way to the bus. Two girls were walking closely behind him, and one of them kept calling the boy's name and teasing him. The boy got midway the fence line, suddenly stopped and turned his head to look across the fence at the lot. The two girls caught up to him and he slammed the teaser to the ground and looked like he was about to jump her—

"Jump her?" Olivia interrupted uncertainly.

"You *know* what I mean, ma'am."

"Oh! Of course, Scott," returned Olivia, amused in spite of herself. The man before her was still checked by the polite restraint which he had often exhibited in her college classroom more than twenty years ago.

"Well, anyway, one of the brothers [one of several male members of the Apostles' Creed congregation who had volunteered to help out at the school] got to him just in time."

"If this 'brother' had been at his post in the first place, the entire incident could have been prevented."

"That's just it! The boy was headed directly toward the man seconds before he attacked, but then he looked back over his shoulder toward your property. It was almost as though something across that fence, something that overpowered his fear of the man standing in front of him, compelled him to act."

"Now, *really*, Scott!" Olivia protested nervously. "The boy probably had just had enough of that girl's taunts. Who is she, by the way?"

"The girl's name is Georgiana Stevenson."

Inwardly Olivia breathed a sigh of relief. Well acquainted with the victim's ever-running mouth, she remembered the times when she herself had wanted to stop its flow with a sharp back-hand slap. This knowledge almost allowed her to dismiss Scott's fears. Almost.

"I know that child; she's one of the students in my Black Heritage class. She is extremely provoking. Of course, that could never excuse what the boy did, and in no way do I condone his actions. As for the land, to the best of my knowledge there is nothing 'wrong' with it. But I'm not the person with whom to discuss the property, even though you've shared with me your desire to buy it to expand the school. I do not own the land. Nathan does. He has for almost seven years now."

"Well, maybe I'll get a chance to speak with him about it at the dinner party tonight." His countenance brightened somewhat. "I'm looking forward to the evening. Thanks for inviting me."

"What gala would be complete without my class crusader?"

"You did use to call me that, didn't you? Looks like I have a ways to go before I save the world," he joked.

"I think that you have done admirably with your part of it, Scott. You are really making a difference in that Bovina community, and I hope that they have the sense to appreciate you and Apostles' Creed." Rising from her chair, Olivia now assumed a lighter tone of voice. "Now, Reverend Kendricks, dismiss yourself. As you well know, I have to prepare for a very special event with some very special people."

"Yes ma'am. I'll see you tonight."

When the door closed behind him, she just stood in the middle of the room trying to order her mind. Hopefully, she had not revealed the real effect that his comments about the land had had on her. Olivia's thoughts tumbled over and collided with one another like frightened beings fleeing before some nebulous yet relentless threat. One course of action did manage to emerge: *"I must talk with Helen."*

Saturday
July 1, 2000
9:00 a.m.

An American Airlines jet glided above the clouds like a regal sliver bird. The sun's rays burnished its metal skin making it glitter against the fathomless blue of midsummer sky. She gazed out the window at a sea of white, billowy clouds tinged with gold. The earth was far beneath them; the sky and sunlight were all around them yet still high above them, always above, calling them up higher. "Just like God," Antoinette whispered to herself.

She directed her attention to the book on her lap and then to the man seated beside her on the aisle. His seat was reclined slightly farther than hers and his eyes were closed. He was not asleep, but blissfully unavailable, having shut out everything except the jazz saxophonist's soothing notes flowing through his headset.

After twenty-two years together, she still loved looking at her husband. He was the handsomest man she knew. She did not mind his tuning out because she knew it meant that he was mellowed. She had seen to that earlier this morning. Her lips curled into a glowing, secret smile as she remembered their time together. After that mysterious phone call, he had been tense and uncommunicative when she had asked what was wrong. Happily, her long experience as his lover had equipped her with the skills to overcome impediments to intimacy, and she had applied those skills very effectively, with his help, of course.

Turning her glance back to her open Bible, her eyes were drawn to the familiar words of the Ninety-first

Psalm: . . . "'Because thou hast made the Lord, which is my refuge, even the most High, thy habitation; There shall no evil befall thee, neither shall any plague come nigh thy dwelling. For He shall give His angels charge over thee, to keep thee in all thy ways. . .'" She ceased to mouth the words and began to meditate. *"So be it. Lord, John needs this. He needs You in His life. I know that You can cut through the confusion in his mind put there in years past by false Christianity, the Nation of Islam, and his own aggressive, pride. Lately I have sensed a struggle within him, so I know that You are at work. I have prayed for him these twenty years,, and I will continue to intercede, for I know that You are faithful and true. Almighty Lord God Jehovah, please save my beloved, and thank You for doing so. In the name of my Lord and Saviour, Jesus Christ, I pray. Amen."*

Shortly after the birth of her twins almost two decades ago, Antoinette had "gotten saved." Born premature, her son and daughter had fought for their lives in the first few days outside her womb. Intense hours spent in the hospital chapel had brought on her moment of crisis. She recalled now how she had uttered what was more like an ultimatum than a prayer, a prayer that had pierced through her husband's anti-Christian rhetoric: *"Jesus, right now I don't care if you're the white man's god or the black man's god or any other race's god. But if you **are** God, then **be** God and let my babies live!"* Her newborns had survived without disability and Antoinette's heart had been won.

Two months later with John standing skeptically but supportively in the congregation of Pearl Street A.M.E. Church, she had confessed Jesus Christ and taken her first communion. The following Sunday the twins had been christened, the result of a considerable concession by their father, as was his daughter's name. He had selected the names *Meji* and *Malika*. *"In honor of our African heritage,"* John had announced. Their mother had agreed, *"Of course, darling, but might not one of their names also show the Christian part of that heritage?"* John's love for her and his appreciation of what she had endured in bearing his children had moved him to reluctantly acquiesce. Thus, their son had taken on the Sierra Leonian name *Meji*, but their daughter had become *Candace*. *"After the great queen of Ethiopia whose servant God saved through the disciple Philip so that he could take the gospel of Jesus Christ to the Ethiopian people, and she will be a virtuous woman of strength and power,"* Antoinette had proclaimed. Candace's father, in spite of himself, had been genuinely pleased.

Barely a week had passed before John Henderson had made good on his premarital pledge *"to get us out of Mississippi as soon as possible."* Jackson State University had bestowed its blessing on the young couple's departure in the form of two new baccalaureate degrees. A fellowship at Howard awaited John, and Washington, D.C. seemed to beckon his psyche, taunting, *"Take me on, if you can!"* He had whisked his wife and children away from the Magnolia State in 1981, and, except for occasional contact with extended family and a few friends, had not given it a backward glance or a caring thought … *"Until now,"* Antoinette's reminiscence brought her abruptly back to the present. Her last thought carried with it a vague sense of apprehension.

Across the aisle another passenger, from force of habit, carefully surveyed the fuselage of the plane. Eyes accustomed to searching, targeting, and assessing scanned the area before them. Ever so often the head turned so that the observer could see the rear, and occasionally a discreet mirror was held at eye level to more closely view activities aft. Looking forward once more, his eyes took in Damaris, Richard and his Haitian nanny, trusted bodyguards and key campaign staff, and the flight attendants. Finally,they rested briefly upon John.

Nathan touched the tips of his fingers together in the form of a triangle and touched the forefingers to his lips. He was deliberating, calculating. *"I was right not to let him exploit my birthday. I will not attempt to capitalize on being born on July 4. For a black man in this country, that date is nothing to celebrate. My father died on that day sixteen years after my birth, and I promised my mother that I would always respect it for his sake, but that's as far as it goes. When the so-called Declaration of Independence was signed, for whom was it intended? Certainly not for the Negroes held in bondage in the colonies. Many of the signers themselves had no problem with being slaveowners. Yet they dared to protest and rebel against British 'tyranny.' The stench of that hypocrisy has lingered for over two hundred years. My purpose is to attack the mindset that is its source and purge this land of it.* [At that point the plane's cabin shuddered slightly, interrupting his contemplation, but the flight attendant smiled at the passengers reassuringly and said, "Just some mild turbulence, folks, don't worry."] *That's nothing compared to the turbulence that's coming to 1600 Pennsylvania Avenue. And, yes, certain persons had better be* **very** *worried."* He stared straight ahead as though peering into the future. The right corner of his mouth rose slightly, but one could not be quite sure if this was an expression of pleasure or of scorn.

Saturday
July 1, 2000
9:30 a.m.

Olivia was relieved that she had decided to have the dinner party catered. This allowed her time to maneuver before going to Jackson International Airport to meet Nathan's flight. She had aimed her vehicle at Clinton, Mississippi, and was speeding like a bullet toward it. The traffic was light, and she counted on the state highway patrolmen being uninterested in a few early motorists. Her specific destination was the assisted living facility which for the past three years had been the residence of her former mother-in-law and Nathan's grandmother. She arrived on the premises a little before 10:00 a.m. *"Record time,"* she thought approvingly as she glanced at her watch. She would take time later to feel guilty about speeding, but right now that was not convenient. The kitchen staff were serving the last of the breakfast patrons in the dining room. As Olivia approached Helen's table, the knowledge that the older woman was now in the moderate stages of Alzheimer's disease pressed upon her. "God, *please* let this be one of her more lucid days," she implored under her breath

An old lady sat contentedly at a table in the middle of the room. Her back was to her daughter-in-law, but Olivia had immediately recognized the crown of white hair tinged with a silvery blue rinse. Mrs. Helen Love Perry wore a simple white high-waisted shift with yellow-gold dasisies embroidered on the bodice. The flower theme was repeated in her necklace and padre sandals. *"Stylish to the last,"* thought Olivia fondly. Helen held the smooth, gold handle of a walking cane loosely in her right hand. She was napping.

Not wanting to startle her, Olivia gently placed a hand on each of her shoulders, leaned down so that she could speak near her ear, and quietly said, "Good morning, Helen." Her mother-in-law opened her eyes and turned her head to see her visitor. A light clicked on behind Helen's eyes, and her whole countenance brightened. Then the light flickered for a split second, "Cassie? Is that you, Cassie?"

"Oh, great! This is not a good start." "No, Helen, dear, I'm not Cassie. Cassie was your daughter. I'm Olivia, your daughter-in-law, Ellis's wife."

Helen leaned forward slightly and recognition again shone in her eyes. "Why, of course, you *are* Olivia. You were my son's Pocahontas, his Indian princess. He was so proud and happy when he first brought you to meet us. How are you, child?"

Olivia conceded that her Native American ancestry had become more pronounced as she had grown older, but she had never seen it in her features in her younger days as Helen seemed to have done. But, this wasn't the time to debate that point.

"I'm well, Mother, and you?"

"I'm blessed."

"I need to talk with you about something. The family land is Nathan's now, and he may want to sell it."

A troubled look clouded Helen's brow. "I hope that he doesn't. That land is his birthright. He is the first-born male in his generation of the Perry family. It's a matter of heritage."

"Yes ma'am, I agree. But that is something that he has to see for himself." Olivia now took a deep breath as a swimmer forced to plunge into muddied, restless waters.

"Mother, tell me about Cassie. Not Cascillia, your daughter, but the *first* Cassie. Tell me about Cassia Marie. Ellis used to say that nobody could tell about her like you could."

"Cascillia, my baby girl, was named after her. I did that because I wanted her to be smart and strong as Cassie was ... She got the land. You knew that, didn't you, dear?"

"But *how*, Mother? She was a freed slave, a widow with young children. *How* could she have done it? It seems impossible."

Helen frowned, trying to remember an idea she'd had. "I don't know ... I think that she must have known something about those people who used to own her. That's why they let her have those first forty acres."

"Blackmail? Blackmail of a plantation owner by his slave?" Olivia asked doubtfully. Her mind raced. "But how would Cassie Mae have the power to do that?"

Helen was looking at her oddly. No, she was gazing past her. By now Olivia knew the signs that preceded the intrusive aberrations of the mind-stealing disease.

"Did Cassie and Ellis come with you, Olivia? I can't see them. Where are they?" Helen asked earnestly.

"Cascillia and Ellis have gone home, Helen," she consoled. "But I believe that both you and I will see them again one day."

The bright look returned to the old woman's eyes, and her daughter-in-law blinked back tears from her own. Olivia rose from her chair, walked behind Helen and softly kissed the top of her head. "They both loved you, Mother. And so do I. Good–bye, for now," she whispered and hurriedly left.

Saturday
July 1, 2000
11:00 a.m.

He wore flawlessly tailored gabardine pants and a white silk shirt. He gave the distinct impression of being a man of means whose wealth had either come hard or had not shielded him from the hardness of life. Perhaps it was the jagged scar that started over his left cheekbone, descended crookedly and stabbed into his moustache. Perhaps it was those piercing, challenging eyes looking out from his swarthy countenance. His black hair was thick and combed back from his face, its texture somewhere between kinky and straight. Jude waited in the penthouse suite of the hotel he had built specifically to accommodate guests of the *Scheherazade*. One of Vicksburg's leading denizens had arranged to meet him to discuss what he had called their "mutual business interests."

Promptly upon the hour, Carlisle Forrest arrived. After exchanging the conventional civilities, the two men seated themselves on opposite sides of a substantial coffee table inset with glittering mosaic tile. The visitor broached the reason for the meeting.

"This is a tremendous opportunity for expansion, Mr. Ramadan. As I mentioned to you earlier, that elevated land overlooking the river, 'The Heights,' as some call it, has tremendous potential. It's a diamond in the rough."

"Be that as it may, Mr. Forrest, I believe there is already a chemical manufacturing concern in operation on the site."

"True. But it's long past its prime and already in a compromised financial condition. My associates and I know from unimpeachable sources that the owners are willing to be bought out to avoid bankruptcy. Our attorneys are already in negotiations."

"How, then, would I take part in this venture?"

"We have planned an extensive development project which includes commercial real estate, a luxury residential area, and (he paused a fraction of a second for effect) a resort complete with a casino and an eighteen-hole championship golf course."

"I see. Quite a bold and ambitious undertaking."

"Your *Scheherazade* is the most successful gaming operation in the area. We could all profit from your obvious expertise in this field. And, is it not true, sir, that you have designs upon that other struggling casino downriver? Well, we intend to encompass it in the project, but we now offer you the opportunity to secure control of it and controlling interest in it."

"Allow me to express my thanks for your faith in my business abilities. But tell me, are there not federal and state regulatory issues, considering the possible contamination of the land from chemical wastes?"

"The Southern Heritage Commission, that is the name of our development group, has legislators and lobbyists in both Jackson and Washington working to circumvent or offset any costly and prolonged state or federal cleanup efforts," responded Carlisle with confident contempt. He felt that government interference in business—on the behalf of the environment or anything else—was a bothersome irritation to be quickly terminated.

"Of course, I might have known that," returned Jude with a slight, sardonic smile. I commend your foresight. However, an opponent in the White House could frustrate your people's efforts."

"Yes. That is possible—if such an opponent ever made it to the White House," said his visitor tersely.

Jude rose from the sofa, walked a few paces from behind the coffee table, turned and stood looking down at his guest. "Please overlook my forthcoming abruptness, Mr. Forrest, but at this point I must ascertain something: In the country of my birth, my forefathers had special castrated male servants, eunuchs, whom they placed over their harems. To outsiders these individuals *looked* the part of strong, masculine defenders. Yet, alas, they had no potency, no life-generating prowess. So, now I must ask you: Do you have *real* decision-making power or do I speak to the Commission's 'eunuch'?"

Anger flashed in Carlisle's eyes. He sprang to his feet. Jude did not move but coolly took the measure of the man before him. The two faced each other for a tense minute.

"You Arab son of a bitch! Desert trash!" Carlisle raged inwardly. He longed to feel the bones in Jude's face cracking beneath the knuckles of his fist. But he was heavily invested in the Heights project and desperately desired its success. Indeed, he wanted this man's money for investment capital, *and* he had yet another proposal in mind, one which he deemed would secure his business interests even better. Thus, with difficulty, he reined in his temper.

"You speak to a person with enough power to make you a separate proposition, Ramadan."

Jude nodded slightly in his direction, thus inviting him to speak further.

"I have researched you, and the effort has yielded invaluable information. It seems that you were quite a busy man before you graced our city with your presence.
You see, I know about the Israeli prison. I know about the murders that put you there. *Jihad*, you called it, right? Well, whatever the name, it resulted in a lot

of dead Jews. I know about your escape and your continued connection with Islamic terrorists."

Here he paused. Jude, seemingly unmoved, neither confirmed or denied anything that was said. He merely waited.

"But most instrumental to my purposes now is that I know you control a network of assassins whose kill rate is very impressive. I want to contract for their services."

Beneath the image of implacable calm, the host bitterly resented this man's attempt to commercialize what he, despite outward appearances, still felt to be a sacred cause. He decided to hear Carlisle out while simultaneously considering punishment for his irreverence.

"Assuming that what you say is true, what target do you have in mind?"

"One worthy of the expertise that I'll be paying for and that I fully expect to receive. You might say that it will be a hit of presidential proportions."

Saturday
July 1, 2000
Sunset

Polished pine cabinets glistened. Carefully arranged copper cookware beamed from a cedar wall rack that had been constructed by the late master of the house.

Countless ebony and silver strands of hair intertwined to form the thick braid approaching the waist of the room's sole occupant. Rays of golden light kissed the woman's reddish brown skin, lending it a rich sheen. The setting sun shone gloriously in Olivia's kitchen. But her thoughts were not glorious. Ever since her conversation with Helen, they had been agitated, restlessly flitting from one possibility to another, trying to reconstruct events from over one hundred years before. Here in this radiant haven, she had sought peace in which to relax and settle her mind before the arrival of the caterers and her guests. Her imagination, however, refused to be quieted.

The dress for the evening was elegant casual. The fare for the dinner party was unpretentious yet highly flavorful (much like the style of the hostess herself): Cornish hens with wild rice, tossed garden salad, seasoned green beans, and cheesecake for dessert, and of course, ice tea. During the meal the conversation had focused on the events of the day. Now, relaxing in the living room, the company was happily reminiscent. Richard could not resist the temptation to explore his father's old room and the attic. In his eagerness he practically dragged Mrs. DuBois, his nanny, up the stairs. The campaign staff was enjoying the hospitality of the Linden Plantation Bed and Breakfast; however, two bodyguards, posted at the front and rear entrances to the house, had accompanied the dinner party guests to the home of Dr. Perry.

The absence of one from the "JSU days" was conspicuous. Olivia explained that she had invited Jude but that he had graciously declined. The reason given was that Independence Day always brought hordes of tourists to the river casinos. He expected huge profits and wanted to be present on the first full day of the holiday weekend to make certain that all went well. As if on cue, the guard stationed at the front door entered the room and handed Nathan an envelope. The congressman opened it and scanned the enclosed card.

"Who brought this?"

"It was delivered by special courier, sir."

The others looked at Nathan inquisitively.

"It's from Jude. He's inviting all of us to be his guests of honor for the Fourth of July festivities on the river Tuesday night."

The invitation received murmurs of pleasant surprise and approval. Yet, John, who had been happily reliving days of full court glory with Scott, felt a cold stone drop to the pit of his stomach, but said nothing. He determined to talk to Nathan about the invitation immediately after the party ended, or sooner if he could do so discreetly.

He was not the only one who wanted a word with the congressman. Scott awaited an opportune moment to speak with him about the Bovina property. Both men would have to wait, however, because Nathan's mother preempted his attention.

"Nathan, would you step into the kitchen with me for a moment? The caterers who have not met you would like to do so."

"Surely, Mother," he replied easily, ever ready to accommodate voters and potential supporters.

"Excuse us for just a few minutes, please," apologized Olivia. "We'll be right back."

"All is well, Dr. Perry," assured her guests contentedly.

Antoinette was sitting beside her husband on the divan. Scott occupied the wing-backed chair to John's right as did Damaris on Antoinette's right side. Scott and Antoinette had begun a conversation about Christian baptism. Damaris listened with interested curiosity. John chose to remain diplomatically silent.

"Since salvation is not in the water, Scott, what difference does it make whether a person is sprinkled or immersed?"

"It makes a difference because of what it signifies. The baptized person identifies with the death of Jesus Christ when he goes under the water, and he identifies with the resurrection of Christ when he emerges from the water."

"This death and resurrection symbolism are important parts of baptism?"

"Crucial, Antoinette, crucial. Baptism also represents dying to one's old self and being raised to a new life in Jesus Christ. It's the outward sign of what has already occurred inwardly when a person accepts Christ as his Savior."

"That's something to seriously think about. Our children were only sprinkled as babies when they were christened, and your teammate and fraternity brother here barely tolerated that." She nudged John in playful reproach.

"Well," Scott addressed his friend with a wry smile, "you've chilled out some since then, man, right?"

"No comment," returned John glibly.

"You know, I've never heard baptism explained like that before. I'm not a Christian, but that was intriguing," Damaris said.
However, it was the speaker more than the words that had captured her attention

"I agree, but I can't take credit for the explanation. The Holy Bible explains itself quite well, if one seeks understanding diligently and earnestly."

The minister smiled politely at Damaris. He was accustomed to the attractiveness of Olivia and Antoinette. The former he respectfully set apart because of her age and position. The latter, always vivacious and charming, was the wife of his best friend. From the time that she had become John's fiancée, he had regarded her as his sister, and even more so since her conversion. But he had just met Damaris tonight. In this stage of initial acquaintance, he discreetly allowed himself the male indulgence of appreciating her physical attributes.
"That's one pretty woman," Scott thought. As the unmarried pastor of a congregation amply supplied

with alluring women, both married and single, he had disciplined himself not to dwell upon such observations. Indeed, one could look without lusting—*if* one did not look too long. Pastor Kendricks kept admiring the view.

The elder Mrs. Perry and her son had returned to the great room on the tail end of Scott's spoken words. They seated themselves on the sofa facing John and Antoinette.

"Has the Reverend Kendricks enthralled all of you with a riveting sermon in our absence?" Olivia asked facetiously.

Her good-natured ribbing was met with light laughter from the group and a somewhat abashed grin from the minister. He decided to turn the tables on his former professor.

"I'm afraid that my expository skills can't compare with yours, Dr. Perry. Do all of you remember her 'niggard speech'?" he asked his former classmates.

There were enthusiastic murmurs to the affirmative.

"That's one of my favorite memories from your class," John asserted.

"Hey, I'm at a disadvantage here," protested Damaris. "I never had the chance to be taught by her, so I never heard this speech. You all know that I did not attend Jackson State University."

"Of course, but we forgave you of that great sin," chirped Antoinette.

"Mom Olivia, help!" appealed Damaris in mock distress. "I sense that they're about to gang up on me."

"I won't have that. You all shall not persecute my daughter-in-law." Then she added teasingly, "Even if up north she was deprived of a *real* college education."

More laughter ensued. Damaris was enjoying herself. Warming to the role of misunderstood outsider, she feigned a gasp at her hostess's words.

"But," Olivia quickly added, "I'll rely on my former students to enlighten her. Tell her what I said that day, class."

Antoinette spoke first: "'*Niggard* is a word meaning "a pathetically covetous, grasping person." It is used in literature by William Shakespeare and other writers to denote an individual of degraded character.'"

Next came Nathan: "'*Negro* is a word referring to a member of the Negroid racial classification just as *Caucasian* refers to the Caucasoid racial classification and *Mongol* [now no longer in use] refers to the Mongoloid racial classification.'"

Then Scott: "'*Nigger* is a corrupted rendering of the word *niggard* perpetrated by pitifully ignorant and/or illiterate persons who, among other deficiencies, cannot spell. Being Negro or black does *not* inherently or automatically connect you to this word, nor does it give you any special ownership of it. Therefore, do not allow anyone, *including yourselves,* to make such a connection or to attribute to you any such ownership.'"

John finished it: "'Niggards/niggers come in all skin colors. Do *not* become one!'"

At this point he and Scot "high fived" each other as though a slam dunk had been plunged through the net.

Damaris listened attentively then thoughtfully responded, "Thank you, class. I am now truly educated."

Saturday
July 1, 2000
9:30 p.m.

As the dinner party on Warrenton Road drew to a close, a few miles upriver, Julia Pembroke Leigh was immersed in the memorabilia locked away in the attic of her mansion inn. She feared no intrusion, for the area was off limits to both patrons and employees. No one else entered except by direct order or express invitation from Mrs.Leigh, who rarely gave either. On the few occasions when she did issue one or the other, she would always be present to supervise or accompany whomever she had selected. This, however, was not one of those times; she was blissfully alone in one of her favorite places.

Prominent members of the Fourth of July River Festival Committee had enlisted her aid for this year's extravaganza. As usual, she had been asked to provide the uniform for the actor who would portray her great grandfather in the reenacted Civil War battle planned as the grand finale of the celebration. Little did the event planners know that for the past five years the uniform lent to them was a well-tailored copy that she'd had prepared. She would present this convincing facsimile to the head of the committee on tomorrow.

Regardless of that deception, there were still more than enough authentic family treasures here for Julia. Presently, she was slowly turning the fragile pages of an album of daguerreotypes. The silver-tinged images possessed a distant, ethereal beauty that stirred a yearning for long-ago, romanticized days. The earliest of the dates written beneath the pictures was 1850. She gazed at the subjects of these early photographs, touched by what she called the "unknowing innocence" captured forever in their faces. Unlike her, they had not known what their fates would be in that damnable war between North and South that even then loomed on the horizon. She mourned for them.

She was about to turn to one of her favorites. It depicted Julius and his wife Regina, flanked respectively by his personal manservant and her personal maidservant standing rigidly as though at attention. The Pembrokes and their children were seated on the front lawn with their magnificent house, the original Cypress Vale, in the background.

But something caught her eye. An individual photograph of Adam, Julius' eldest son and her grandfather, had apparently slipped from its place and was protruding out from between pages she had yet to turn. Julia carefully fingered the edges of the pages until she reached the place where the picture stuck out. She then opened the book completely. There were the remnants of hardened glue that had released Adam's image. Curiously, however, a folded sheet of yellowed paper stuck to the page where the daguerreotype had rested. Gingerly detaching it, she opened the paper. It was a letter. Delighted over this discovery, she began to read.

****

Revelation

The Fourth Day
(Traitors and Truth)

Sunday
July 2, 2000
11:00 a.m.

Sunday dawned hot and sticky. Bethel African Methodist Episcopal Church was packed wall-to-wall with the *faithful*, the *grateful*, and the *curious*. The faithful would have been present regardless; rain or shine, when the church doors opened, they were there because they were genuinely committed. The grateful had miraculously survived hellish life experiences and dared not seem unthankful by being absent. The curious showed up to see what would happen, as they did from Sunday to Sunday. This latter group was out in force today. Their appetite for the sensational had been tantalized by the much publicized attendance of presidential candidate, Nathan Sundiata Perry.

The pastor had asked Nathan to briefly address the congregation after the sermon. Now, seated on the first pew of the center aisle with Damaris and Richard beside him, he reviewed the notes for his speech. But his usual meticulousness was impaired. Intrusive recollections of his confrontation with Olivia on the night before persisted. When his mother had asked him to come into the kitchen, it had not been only to meet members of the catering staff. Already having cleaned up and packed up their equipment, they departed not more than five minutes after his appearance, proudly carrying dinner napkins that bore his freshly scribbled autograph. As he had suspected, Olivia wanted to speak with him privately. The words that had passed between them now replayed themselves in his mind, disrupting his concentration.

"Nathan, I'm very proud of you. You've accomplished so much," she began.

"Thank you, Mother. But of course I couldn't help myself. I inherited such dynamic genes!" They both smiled at that.

"Do you feel that you are ready for the presidency if you win it?"

"More than ready."

"Son, you would galvanize the history of the United States if you were to be elected."

"As you have said so many times, 'Black men have made history in this country since its conception, but their contributions have been credited to others or have been grossly ignored.' Well, I can't be ignored. Not now and not in November."

"You have called for inclusion and unity in your campaign platform. Nathan, is that truly your heart?"

"My heart is something that Father and you helped to shape. So you already know that our people are dear to it. I see what we are; I know what we need; and I envision what we can be."

"When you say 'our,' people, do you mean the American people? You must. It cannot be otherwise, Sundiata, no matter what Ellis and I strived for and taught you, it cannot be otherwise. The controlling forces will not tolerate a United States president bent on black power. They will kill you."

"To answer your question, yes, our people are most definitely American. None other have paid as costly a price for this nationality as we have. Slavery, lynchings, burnings, rapings, dehumanizing discrimination, government-sanctioned segregation,— all in 'the land of the free and the home of the brave'! Who more than we have earned the title 'American'? As for the 'controlling forces,' forgive my language, but they can go to hell."

"You are my only child. No cause is worth your life!"

"What is my life worth if I have no belief for which I am willing to die?"

"*I* am not willing for you to die! If you won't consider me, think of your wife and son."

"I think of them constantly." At this point he placed a hand on each of her shoulders and looked closely into her face. "And you and I both know that I probably will soon be taken from them, no matter what I do or don't do as president."

He let his words penetrate, which they did, quickly. Olivia's eyes widened in alarm. Desperate words of protest and denial sprang to her lips.

"No, mother. Just listen. My father, my grandfather, and my great grandfather barely survived forty years on this earth. I will be forty on Tuesday. You have not mentioned my birthday. I know that you didn't forget it. Were you afraid to bring it up?" He smiled at her understandingly. "Not talking about it won't stop the inevitable. I know that my time may be short, but I *will* lay the groundwork for black supremacy in this country before I die. This will be *my* legacy for my family to cherish after I am gone.

[Remember how short my time is: wherefore Hast thou made all men in vain? – Psalm 89:47]

He leaned forward and kissed her cheek, brushing away the tear glistening there. "Now, let's go back and rejoin the party."

Olivia prudently regained her composure as he'd known that she would. Following her brisk strides, he knew without seeing her face that her countenance now displayed confident graciousness with no hint of emotional distress, for that was her way.

"That's it, Mother. Always present the image of you that you want to etch into the minds of people. Then *you* have the control," he thought.

"… I now present to you Congressman Nathan Sundiata Perry. Let's welcome him as he comes."

The minister's words broke into his reflections. Applause burst forth like a thunderclap around him as the congregation stood and called his name. He rose from the pew, strode to the left side of the altar, mounted the steps to the pulpit and then moved to the lectern.

"Thank you, thank you, my friends. Indeed, we are blessed to be here this morning. Please be seated."

The clapping gradually subsided, and there was a general rustling movement as the audience took their seats. When all was quiet, Nathan gazed solemnly over the people and began:

"*One* nation under God. This is our creed. This is our destiny …"

Sunday
July 2, 2000
3:00 p.m.

Scott rose from his desk chair, stretched, and began to walk slowly and thoughtfully about his office. To his surprise, Olivia Perry had shown up for morning worship service at Apostles' Creed Victory Church. He had naturally assumed that she would be present at Bethel to support her son. After the benediction and dismissal, she had lingered while he fellowshipped with his members. Laughing, shaking hands, hugging the small children that ran up to him, he had truly been in his element. Scott had greeted each person warmly, sometimes giving encouragement, sometimes administering gentle admonishment. It was his sincere desire that all members felt special and cared for by God through their pastor.

As the last of his flock were exiting the sanctuary, Olivia had walked resolutely toward him. Her usual poised cordialness had seemed somewhat strained and could not entirely mask the undercurrent of urgency. After she had commended him on his sermon, she had asked him to meet her at the Warren County Court House on Monday morning. She needed his help investigating Nathan's property, *"For your sake as well as his,"* she had added emphatically. Scott had then informed her that before leaving her house the previous night, he and Nathan had arranged to meet on the site on Monday evening to discuss the sale. Though she had maintained her outward composure, he could tell that this news increased her agitation. He smiled reassuringly, saying that he would be at the court house and that he was sure that they would find all things to be well. Olivia had thanked him and departed.

Now as he continued pacing, he chided himself for not working on the message for the evening service which would begin three hours hence. That had been his intention when he had come into his study. His Bible still lay open on his desk, turned to the first chapter of the Book of Acts from which would come his text. But he had been unable to concentrate on the scriptures. His mind kept returning to Nathan Perry's land—his high hopes for it and his illogical wariness of it. "I need to pray," he asserted out loud.

Scott knelt before the window that faced the problematic vacant lot. He had always found it difficult to abruptly fling himself into prayer, pouring out the contents of the soul and spirit to God. Rather, he usually made himself stop and think about what he wanted to say, as he did now. Once he had thought out what was on his heart, he began.

"Lord, what is it? What's wrong? Why have there been so many incidents of strife among the students? Why do I have a check in my spirit each time that I make a move to purchase the property beside us? I only want to fulfill the charge that *You* laid upon me and that I gladly accepted. I want to create a place where underprivileged children can be rooted and grounded in the Word of God and where they can be diligently taught the accumulated knowledge of Man. What is this opposition that I feel? You said in Your Word, 'If any of you lack wisdom, let him ask of God, that giveth to all men liberally, and upbraideth not; and it shall be given him.' Well, Father, I'm asking. and I know that You are faithful and true to give liberally. Thank you for doing it. In the name of the Lord Jesus Christ, I pray. Amen."

He waited. He "listened" for the familiar voice that spoke quietly yet firmly *within* him but that did not come *from* him. But there was only the sound of his steady breathing. Scott got to his feet and sat back down in his desk chair, still in a state of expectancy. His eyes fell upon the pages of the open Bible. He scanned the words in the first chapter, and one kept snagging his attention. It was a name: **Judas**.

(. . . the Lord. . . will bring to light the hidden things of darkness, and will make manifest the counsels of the hearts . . . - ICorinthians 4:5)

****

Resolution

The Fifth Day
(Partnerships, Perils
and . . . Proselytizing?)

Monday
July 3, 2000
9:00 a.m.

"Why is he really coming here? To gloat? To intimidate me?"

Ever since Nathan Perry had communicated his wish to pay her a visit while he was in Vicksburg, she had pondered on his ulterior motive. Congresswoman Cecilia Sherman was still smarting over her loss to Perry at the Freedom Party's National Convention. Battling through the melee of the primaries, they had emerged as the two front-runners. With that distinction had come the pressure to become adversaries.

In retrospect, she acknowledged that she had been the first to succumb to this pressure. To use the flippant terminology of the media, Sherman had "thrown the 'race card.'" Pointing to Nathan's younger days as what the press had called a "black militant," she had suggested that Congressman Perry "may not have the interests of the **whole** nation at heart." He had swiftly retaliated by playing what could be called the "gender card," hinting that a woman who had just come through a vicious and very public divorce "may have a **vindictive, unhealthy** perspective of the male gender" which prompted her to accuse him now and which would undoubtedly taint her judgment if she were to become the nation's chief executive officer.

Cecilia had not known at the time (and still did not know) that it was John Henderson, Perry's campaign manager, who held the *real* trump card. His investigators had unearthed it, and,indeed, it was damning. John had held the information in reserve, assuring Nathan that, *"She may have struck the first blow, but I guarantee that with this, we will draw first and last blood and knock her out of the race."*

So John had held back, waiting to strike at the pivotal moment. What did he have on Cecilia? At the time, Nathan had not concerned himself with that. Indeed, smearing his opponent had proven to be unnecessary. A tidal surge of popular support shortly before the Convention had propelled him far beyond her. Yet, John and Nathan had agreed that in the very near future the information must be "shared" with Cecilia just in case she needed to be kept in check.

Cecilia remembered with chagrin the wild excitement of the night that Congressman Perry had won the nomination. "Perry mania" had electrified the air and no one seemed insulated against it. Then, as though his black presence in the position of Freedom Party Presidential Candidate was not defiant enough, he had defied history even further by declining to immediately name a running mate. However, he had vowed to do so expeditiously "after considering the stellar array of capable men and women in the Party."

"Could that be it? Is that why he's coming here?" She marveled at the possibility, but by no means did she reject it.

Monday
July 3, 2000
10:00 a.m.

They had been at the Chancery Court House since shortly before it opened at eight o'clock. As the clerk had

77

approached the double doors of the tax assessor's office with key in hand, he had been surprised to see two persons already there waiting to be admitted—a man, no older than forty and dressed in clergyman's attire, and a handsome matron in her early sixties with flowing salt and pepper hair. The woman had seemed vaguely familiar to him, not from personal acquaintance but through the ceaseless efforts of the ubiquitous media. They both were apparently quite eager to enter.

He had barely positioned himself behind the counter when the man had walked up and asked, "Just how far back do your property records go, sir?"

Pleased to be addressed as "sir," the clerk had affably drawled, "Well, Reverend, we have documents dating as far back as the early 1800's."

"Splendid," the woman had replied with crisp efficiency while extracting a sheet of paper from her briefcase. "Will you please direct us to the records of ownership for this piece of property?" She had handed the slight, balding man the paper containing the lot number and other identifying information.

The clerk had ushered Scott and Olivia into a room where huge books in metal casings were arranged consecutively by years on bookcases built into the walls. The years that each volume encompassed were indicated on the spine of each book. In the center of the room, several long wooden tables were aligned in straight rows with chairs drawn under the sides of each. Scott had pulled back a chair for his former professor and, one at a time, had taken two mammoth volumes from one of the bookshelves. Olivia had turned to the clerk with a smile and said, "Thank you," thus politely dismissing him. After advising them that the office would be closing early because of the upcoming holiday, he had left them to their work.

Some two hours later, the two of them were still there, and their labor had borne fruit.

"Let's review what we know so far," suggested Scott.

Olivia scanned documents she had brought in her briefcase. "Vicksburg was incorporated as a municipality in 1825. Seven years later Justin Pembroke bought one hundred acres about fifteen miles east of what were then the city limits. That land was the seed of the Cypress Vale Plantation. Justin's eldest son Julius inherited the property. Under his hand it reached its full glory, covering nearly one thousand acres in the late 1850's to early 1860's. In 1863 Ulysses S. Grant marched his troops in from the east, bent on capturing Vicksburg and thus freeing the Mississippi River from Confederate control. Parts of the plantation were ravaged during battles at Champion Hill and at the Big Black River Bridge. But the majority of the land was undamaged."

Scott observed, "From July 1863 to July 1865 there is a gap in these records. When they resume, they include the Perry deed to forty acres formerly belonging to Cypress Vale. From then on, the Pembrokes retained possession of the remaining plantation lands until James Pembroke sold it all to the Southern Heritage Commission in 1986. Dr. Perry, if there is some problem with this property, the key to revealing it is hidden within that two-year lapse."

"I agree with you, Scott. It's no surprise to me that those years mark a break in the property records; conditions at the time were in a state of upheaval. Let me briefly revert to the role of history professor to put things in proper perspective: On July 4, 1863, Vicksburg was officially surrendered to Grant after a 46-day siege. By July, 1865, the Civil War had been officially over for three months. In April of that year, Robert E. Lee, commanding general of the Confederate armies, had surrendered to General Grant at Appomattox Court House, Virginia.

"The nation was faced with the rebuilding of the South. Thus, the Reconstruction Era began. The newly restructured and federally backed governments of the Southern states offered aid to railroads and other industries and worked to attract investment money from the North, but land ownership remained the basis for independence, riches, and influence in the South. Bitter, dispossessed whites struggling against starvation owned no land and no longer could they own the means of cultivating it—black men, women, and children. This created a hostile environment for freed Negroes fortunate enough to obtain property. Even with the protection of federal troops, the danger persisted. The fact that Cassia Marie Perry, an ex-slave and widow, acquired and kept those first forty acres is phenomenal."

"That was _miraculous_." thought Scott. But aloud he said, "Do you have any idea how she was able to do it?"

Olivia hesitated for a moment, unwilling to voice Helen's idea because of her mother-in-law's fragile mental state. "My late husband's mother thinks that she blackmailed her way into owning that land. She believes that the land and protection were pay-offs for her silence about something."

"What crime during or after the war could be severe enough to force a Southern rebel to cater to the will of a slave?"

Even as he spoke, again—but this time stronger, more intense—the name resounded in his mind: *"Judas."*

"Scott? What's wrong?"

He looked at Olivia resolutely. "It was treason, Dr. Perry. Cassie Mae knew about someone's betrayal, and I sense that we had better find out whose it was."

**Monday
July 3, 2000
4:00 p.m.**

Many of the students at Apostles' Creed Christian Academy resided in the neighborhood where the school was located and were frequent visitors to the campus for what had become locally known as SASR, or Supervised After School Recreation. From 4:00 p.m. to 6:00 p.m. on weekdays from September through July, children ages six through twelve could gather in a safe, clean, outdoor setting under prudent adult supervision. Structured activities were offered or one could engage in "free style" playing on the recreational equipment. Pastor

Kendricks wanted to offer SASR clients an outlet for youthful energy that was "neither illegal or immoral."

On this particular afternoon, something special was afoot. The news had spread across the playground like the sweet aroma of backyard barbeque: Pastor Kendricks, yes, the preacher, was going one-on-one in a basketball match-up with an ex-NBA star from Washington, D.C.! (the error in communicating John's status had freely flowed from Georgiana Stevenson, that ever-gushing fountain of misinformation).

As though jet propelled, every male child instantaneously appeared at the basketball court. Most of the girls were not far behind. The church volunteers serving as SASR supervisors soon found themselves with no one to supervise, a situation which delighted them since they wanted to see the game also.

ACCA's basketball court was host to two players entering the prime of their lives. Perhaps there would not be the lightning speed or the aerial dynamics of youth. These had been preempted by grace and smoothness of motion, by studied shrewdness of action, and by the confidence of having physical power under mental control. A church elder served as referee. He threw the ball straight above their heads. Both men leaped to capture the spherical prize. John landed with it secure in his grasp, drove toward the goal, and scored.

The opponent received the praise due the first scorer, and Richard Perry cheered ecstatically for his "Uncle Johnny." But as far as the academy students and neighborhood children were concerned, it was a Kendricks crowd. Moreover, they were happily astonished to see the minister in this new light. While the boys focused mainly on his moves, some of the older girls whispered excitedly about other aspects. Scott wore sweat pants, Nike's, and a blue and white JSU sleeveless t-shirt.

"Girl, do you see Pastor's muscles? I didn't know preachers even had any!"

"And look! He's got those brands on his arm. My sister's boyfriend goes to Jackson State and he has the same ones. That's Alpha Phi Alpha. The guys who pledge get those symbols branded on them when they go over."

"That means that Pastor is a frat brother! At his age? And he's a preacher? O-o-oh! I can't believe it. He must have got special permission from God to do *that* !"

"I think that D.C. guy is an Alpha, too."

The young ladies' interest was shared by other female onlookers some years their senior.

"They're really good," observed Damaris in surprised admiration.

"Yes, they are. You should have seen them in college." At that moment John made a lay-up, and Antoinette sprang to her feet. "Woooh! Go, baby!" she screamed while clapping.

Mrs. Henderson was truly stunning in a deep scarlet sun dress. The bodice flattered her shapely bosom, and the finely pleated skirt gracefully draped and shaped the rest of her figure. Ultra thin streaks of gold lined the spaces between the pleats and subtilely embellished the scarlet cloth. A matching parasol shielded her from the sun's unrelenting rays. Beneath it, her meticulously spaced black braids hung down well past her shoulder blades and were elegantly adorned with minute scarlet and gold beads. The sunblock had given her mahogany skin a warm glow.

Seated beside her and sharing the generous shade of her parasol, Mrs. Perry reclined in stylish refinement. She wore cool, yellow pastel, her sleeveless silk blouse matching her skirt perfectly. The soft leather belt hugging her waist had tiny pearls sewn into it at regular intervals. Earrings and bracelet matched these gems, as did a small brooch at the base of her V-shaped collar. Her brownish-black tresses were swept to one side of her face and gathered in a ponytail that rested upon her breast. She was the color of café au lait, coffee and milk in equal amounts.

The two of them were a pleasing sight. Antoinette was eagerly watching the game, as she should have been, for her husband played in it. Damaris was eagerly watching the game, as perhaps, she shouldn't have been, for hers did not.

"Nathan really likes basketball," his wife felt obligated to say, "but he doesn't get a chance to play much."

"By the way, where is he? John said that he'd be joining us out here."

"Oh, he will. He and Pastor Kendricks have some business to discuss. But first he had a late lunch meeting with Cecilia Sherman."

"Really? Well, maybe he's going to make peace with her. Things got pretty nasty between them in the primaries. I don't approve of mud-slinging tactics. But Ms. Sherman did attack first. Nathan gave back as good as he got, though. Anyway, I hope that they can reconcile their differences. A divided party doesn't win elections."

"May I ask you something?" Damaris ventured.

"You surely may," returned Antoinette amiably.

"This is off the subject, but I want to know. You really seem to have nailed the 'loving wife/devoted mother' role. Don't you want something of your own apart from John and the twins? Haven't you ever desired your own career and accomplishments?"

"I have been there, and I have done that, Damaris," Antoinette said resolutely. "Maybe one day I'll go back to it, but right now I'm very content as I am."

"Okay, there's something else I've wondered about. You're a Christian; John definitely is not. From what I can tell, you are very serious about your faith. So, how do you manage to reconcile that with your marriage to him?"

"My goodness, you are full of questions this afternoon, aren't you? Well, I rely upon the word of God to guide me in my marriage. The Bible says that even though my husband is an unbeliever, if he is content to stay with me, then I am to stay with him and live as a godly woman before him. Doing so is my best means of winning him to the Lord and the best way of blessing our household with peace."

"Both Nathan and I are non-Christians."

"And you two are all right with that?"

"I guess."

"Even so, the Bible sets forth sound principles for a happy marriage, whether you're Christian or not. I can summarize them in this sentence: The chief need of a husband is to be *honored* and *respected*; the chief need of a wife is to be *cherished* and *protected*."

"I'll remember that."

Explosive cheers erupted from the children. Scott had executed a slam dunk.

"All right now, Rev!" shouted Antoinette with the sororal supportiveness that she had grown accustomed to showing him.

"Pastor Kendricks...Scott... seems to be truly dedicated to his ministry. So, has he ever been married ?"

"No, he hasn't." She looked at Damaris. "Why do you ask?"

"Oh. .. well, no particular reason ...," she was visibly flustered.

"Yes, there is, Damaris," Antoinette said understandingly. "Quite naturally, when a woman, married or not, sees an attractive, respectable, man of Scott's age, she wonders if there is or has been a special woman in his life. There's nothing wrong with wondering about that."

"He's not a homosexual is he?" Damaris's curiosity got the better of her propriety.

"Hardly! Back when the three of us were at J-State, and John and I became engaged, Scott stayed "single" and available—very available. He was a star athlete, a member of Alpha Phi Alpha fraternity, and a dean's list scholar. Believe me, women were falling all over themselves trying to get to him. He was no saint, but he treated every girl he dated with respect. And now, of course, he's a Christian minister of the Gospel. Both our Bible *and* your Torah condemn homosexuality as an abomination. Scott Kendricks is no hypocrite.

"Then I suppose that he just has not found the right woman?" she persisted.

"Right now I don't think he's looking. He's come a long way since those college days. Now he's a man with a mission," Antoinette turned to look Damaris full in the face, "much like your own husband."

"Nathan is ... different," came the quiet response.
"Well, he *is* and he *isn't*," countered Antoinette. "True, he hasn't been into sports and athletics to the extent that John and Scott have; his interests and personality led him a different way. That's why he went

on to law school and later gravitated to politics. But the three of them have this in common: They think deeply; they feel passionately; and they act with conviction. Once when John spoke to me about their activist days in college, he said, *'Ann, we were mind, heart, and will: the mind conceives a thing; the heart believes it; the will achieves it. I was the mind; Scott, the heart; and Nathan, the will.'* People couldn't understand why he stepped down from heading his firm to manage Nathan's campaign, but it was no surprise to me. John knows that Nathan can realize the beliefs and goals that they share. Your husband is a man of purpose, Damaris, and men of purpose need women of virtue to stand beside them and to be supportive."

"But how can I do that?" she asked frustratedly. "So often he seems to be in a place that I can't reach. Besides, some of John's beliefs I don't *want* Nathan to share. Forgive me for saying so, Antoinette, but your husband sometimes seems quite racially prejudiced."

"Don't confuse racial prejudice with racial pride, Damaris. I constantly pray that John,too, will see that distinction. And as for your being unable to reach Nathan, well, maybe that's because you need to let *yourself* be reached by Someone who knows both you and Nathan intimately and has your best interests at heart."

"Come on, now, Antoinette. I see where you're going with this. I'm not religious, and even if I were, my family background is Jewish, not Christian."

Antoinette smiled and responded, "The Person to Whom I refer also was not religious and *His* family background was Jewish, too."

A shrill blast from the referee's whistle signaled that the game was over. It had ended in a tie.

"We'll finish our conversation later. Right now I have to go and celebrate the two victors. Oh look, Nathan's car is pulling up. I'll pass on your congratulations to John and Scott. I know that you'll want to properly greet your *own* man *first.*"

Her clear emphasis did not escape Damaris. She suddenly felt a sense of friendship and something else- maybe gratitude?- toward Antoinette. She called after her, "Hey, what field was your career in before you took this—sabbatical?

"Oh, didn't I tell you?" Antoinette called back laughingly as she strode toward center court, "Psychology!"

Monday
July 3, 2000
5:00 p.m.

The only thing racing faster than her pulse was her mind. *She* could be Vice President of the United States! She looked at herself closely in the dresser mirror. The familiar Scotch-Irish features were reflected back at her. There were the same green eyes, the same abundant auburn hair, the same light sprinkling of freckles on her nose. Yet, a universe of change had occurred. To reassure herself that she was not delusional, she mentally replayed the events of that afternoon.

They sat drinking lemonade on the veranda of her home right outside Bolton, Mississippi. Her superb cook, a long-time family employee known venerably as "Ms.Ida Mae," had prepared a light but delectable lunch which they had just heartily consumed.

"Thank you, ma'am, for the marvelous food! There's nothing like Mississippi cooking. I wish I could find salmon like that in Washington or Philadelphia," he complimented Ida as she refilled their glasses. He was so effortlessly debonair, truly a charming man, when he wanted to be.

"Well, son, you need to get back home more often. You've been gone from us for some time now, but we been hearin' about you. Keep up the good work. Cecilia, honey, will you be needin' anything else? I'd like to tidy up the kitchen and get home a little earlier this evening. I got family coming in for the Fourth."

"No, Ms. Ida, we'll be fine. Please be careful driving home. Enjoy your holiday and don't forget to save me and the children some of your special barbequed ribs!"

He rose to open the screen door for the cook and closed it behind her. Then he turned to address his hostess. "Thank you for your hospitality, Congresswoman Sherman. You have been quite gracious, especially since I, more or less, invited myself into your home today. But this only reaffirms the decision that I have made."

She grudgingly admired the ease with which he shifted from grass-roots amiability to political expediency.

"We both want the Freedom Party to run a winning ticket in November. The country is ripe for radical change; my

*winning the Party's nomination is undeniable proof of that. I
say let's continue to rock the status quo and give the people not
only their first black President, but also their first female Vice
President. So, will you be my running mate in the General
Election?"*

*Fireworks were explodimg in her ego, but she managed to
express only surprised appreciation. "Why me?" she asked.*

*"Why not you? You have courage and a sense of fair
play, unless, of course, you feel threatened as you did at one
point in your former campaign. Even so, I can't fault you for
your survival instinct, and I make no apology for mine. Also,
your efforts in Congress to pass or to defeat certain pieces of
legislation show your concern for your constituency. Finally
and most importantly, there is strength in unity. Two former
opponents coming together present a solid, unified Party to the
American people. Now, do you accept my offer?"*

"I do, sir."

He offered his hand which she readily accepted.

*"Thank you, Cecilia. I'm very happy to have you onboard.
I'll make a formal announcement at the Independence Day
gathering tomorrow at Vicksburg's Old Court House Museum.
You will be able to attend, won't you?"*

*"Of course," she replied with appropriate enthusiasm while
inwardly she vowed, "Nothing short of my untimely death will
stop me from being there!"*

*"Excellent! One of my staff will brief you later today. Well
then, I will see you on tomorrow, Ms. Vice President," he
smiled at her confidently and then departed.*

Yes, it was all true. "Vice President Cecilia Sherman,"
she allowed herself to say aloud. "I *do* like the sound of
that. And as the saying goes, I'll be 'only one heartbeat
away from the presidency'! ... But speaking of 'hearts,'

Nathan, what's really in yours? You *talk* a convincing game, but can I trust you? I wonder."

If she could have read his mind as he walked to his car after taking leave of her, her wonder might have changed to apprehension.

"Now my image is complete," he had thought triumphantly.

(The heart is deceitful above all things, and desperately wicked: who can know it? – Jeremiah 17:9)

Monday
July 3, 2000
6:00 p.m.

The two of them strolled leisurely along the fence line between the two properties—preacher and politician, minister and statesman, Scott and Nathan. Each, no doubt, wondered what role he should play in this possible real estate transaction. Scott knew how much he needed the Perry land; Nathan knew how tempted he was to sell it.

They also had to realize that the two of them had never actually been close friends. Oh, yes,"back in the day" (he expression used to refer to their college years) they had been friendly acquaintances. But that had been a spin-off from their mutual association with John, the eldest of the three. John and his athletic prowess, John and his incisive wit, John and his intense passion for black empowerment and the dangerous associations which that passion generated. He had represented certainty and conviction to them, a point from which each younger man could orient himself.

And they had both needed that. Scott was from a small town in Iowa and had come to Jackson State University on a basketball scholarship. He had struggled with "culture shock" and appreciated the genuine camaraderie easily offered by John, his assigned roommate. Just when he was "coming of age," Nathan had lost his father, Dr. Ellis Perry, a prominent educator and civil rights activist. As a college student, he had fought to reconcile the urge to go his own way with the duty to carry on his father's work. His mother, Olivia, had shared her husband's beliefs and was an influential instructor on campus, but in the wake of his father's death she had stated with crystal clarity that Nathan was her beloved son, *not* her protégé.

"I want you to be a proud black man who actualizes his potential <u>and</u> lives to enjoy the fullness of his life. This cause of equality has wrenched one martyr from my heart. I <u>will</u> <u>not</u> prepare for it another." She had been adamant.

Thus, John had filled a void in both their lives and had been the basis of their association. Now, twenty years later, how were they to relate to each other? Their mutual friend and mentor had e xcused himself on account of a "pressing matter" that required his attention. He had escorted the ladies, who looked forward to an afternoon of shopping and antiquing, back to Vicksburg in one of the staff vehicles. Richard, however, had opted to remain behind with his father.

Scott had already given Nathan a tour of the Apostles' Creed complex which faced the westbound corridor of the interstate and was separated from it by a frontage road. They had begun with the academic building at the rear, the north end, and had proceeded in a clockwise direction to take in the administrative offices, media center, church sanctuary, and thrift store. Their course ended on the academy playground adjacent to the fence that separated the complex from Nathan's property. Here they had lost the younger Perry who, ecstatic to have the entire play area to himself, ran jubilantly toward the nearest recreational edifice. His father yelled after him to stay where he could see him. Richard yelled back, "Yes, sir!" and sped on his way.

Looking at the land across the fence, Scott pointed to several areas and told what structures he would erect there. Nathan listened intently.

"This place is quite impressive. You've achieved a great deal."

"Thank you. I've been richly blessed. And what *you've* achieved is truly amazing. You're making history."

"You're referring to 'Congressman Nathan Sundiata Perry, Freedom Party Presidential Candidate'?" Nathan asked with a quirky smile.

"Well, of course. But tell me this, man. How did you come by that combination in your first and middle names? I've wondered about it since I began hearing people discussing you on the news," Scott asked jokingly.

It was now apparent that each man felt that he did not have to be on his guard with the other. They had both begun to relax.

"Oh, yeah, that. See, *Nathan* was given to me in honor of my father's close friend, Nathan Steinberg. They worked together in the Mississippi Project back in 1966 when the Student Nonviolent Coordinating Committee launched its campaign to register blacks to vote. Steinberg was killed for that," he said quietly.

"Those were rough times."

"Exactly. Now, *Sundiata* was my mother's doing. Sundiata ruled the Mali Empire in West Africa during the mid- thirteenth century and made it one of the largest and wealthiest domains in the region. He was known as the 'son of the Lion.'"

"Those names and the men behind them—that's a lot to live up to. But you've represented them well," Scott sincerely observed.

"I appreciate your saying that. There are times, though, when I would trade places with you and others like you. Your efforts have produced tangible results that trace back directly to you. Mine have not. It's one thing to legislate; it's quite another to create."

"Nathan, generations of African Americans have lived and died hoping to one day see a black man rise to the point that you have reached. What value do you place on a deferred hope fulfilled?"

"You make a good minister, Scott. I stand corrected. Thank you."

"You're welcome. Now, how do you feel about selling me your land so that I can continue to be a good minister and expand this ministry that has been entrusted to me?"

Nathan was silent for a moment. A slight frown fleetingly creased his brow but then vanished. Finally, as though struggling against an unhappy fate, he spoke.

"You've built a facility to develop our future—the minds, and bodies of our children. Few things are as important as that, and I would love to contribute to it. But … I can't sell you this property."

"What's wrong, Nathan?"

He looked away for a moment and breathed a brief sigh. "Do you know what it feels like to be under the gun every day of your life, to be always pitted against a ticking clock?"

"Every man has known that feeling, but not many can stand it as a constant pressure."

"*I do,*" Nathan said soberly. "Look, I know that you won't understand this, but if I give up this land that my father left me and that I am supposed to pass on to my son, it would mean that I have given up, that I couldn't beat that clock."

Scott looked perplexed. "I'm not following you."

"All right, then let me ask you this. As a minister, do you believe in curses?"

"Yes," Scott replied firmly.

"That was quite definite. You're that sure?"

"I can't deny or debate the existence of something that the word of God confirms. But I also know this: The Word says that 'the curse causeless shall not come.' That means that there has to be a reason for a curse. Once that reason, that cause is discovered, it must be brought under the blood of Jesus Christ. Thus, the curse will be expiated."

Nathan looked closely at Scott who returned his gaze evenly. "You've thought about this before, haven't you? I mean, before I ever brought it up?"

"Yes, I have," Scott admitted. "Something's very wrong with your land, Nathan. And maybe whatever judgment you feel is upon *you* is connected to *it*."

"What you said about killing the curse, does that apply to everybody?"

"It applies to every true saint of Jesus Christ," Scott stipulated.

"I don't fit into that category," retorted Nathan, "and I will not fake it to try to save myself from my own superstitious weakness."

Suddenly, a sharp cry from behind them caused both men to turn around.

Richard lay crumpled on the ground as an empty swing moved to and fro in the breeze.

Monday
July 3, 2000
8:00 p.m.

The docks were unaccustomedly busy for a Monday evening, but with good reason. Preparations for the big Independence Day celebration had carried over from earlier in the day. Indeed, many revelers had already gotten a head start on their dining and gambling. The grand dining room of the Cypress Vale Mansion Inn and the main deck of the *Scheherazade* riverboat casino were but two of the riverfront establishments aflame with activity. Yet, elsewhere on the premises of these two places something beyond robust partying was occurring, something secretive, and thereby, sinister.

John jogged smoothly and confidently along the cobblestone streets lined with picturesque eateries, boutiques, and specialty shops, each with its own distinctive flair. These riverfront stores were the result of the Main Street Project, the business community's ambitious campaign to revitalize downtown Vicksburg. He easily maneuvered around ambling tourists. The memory of his morning workouts in Georgetown brought an appreciative smile to his lips. He had already covered more than a mile on Washington Street and had not even broken a sweat.

A few feet beyond the lively thoroughfare, the Mississippi River lay majestically in the twilight. The dark waters glittered briefly with liquid gold, a reflection of the light from the departed sun. Cloaked in dusk, it undulated ever southward, extending beyond the bridge that spanned its width then continuing its odyssey to the beckoning Atlantic. Frozen in time on the looming bluffs and ridges overlooking the river's course, cannon kept vigil as they had 137 years ago when North and South had clashed in the Civil War.

John's eyes followed the shimmering waves as the water flowed past his chosen destination. Nathan Perry's campaign workers, indeed even the employees of his own firm, might have had difficulty recognizing him on this evening. He wore black athletic shoes, dark jeans, and a black t-shirt. The shirt hung down several inches below the waistband of his jeans. A cap was pulled down low upon his brow.

Deftly he descended the sharply sloped paved driveway leading to the parking lot for the *Scheherazade*. In a corner of the lot a good distance away from the riverboat itself, he spotted three men. Crouching and using the rows of vehicles to hide himself, he drew nearer and nearer until he could hear their conversation and even glimpse their faces. His focus was not the man seeming to give the orders but the two men receiving them: One was Sudanese, the other, Syrian. All three men spoke Arabic. Though his knowledge of the language was limited, he recognized certain utterances immediately: *Bukra*, "tomorrow"; *Laa budda min*, "It is absolutely necessary"; and *Laa takhaf*, "no fear."

Then two of the speakers moved swiftly away from the third and headed down toward the riverbank, one veering to the north, the other to the south. In one smooth motion, John reached beneath his shirt, pulled the Glock 27 from his waistband, stood up straight and targeted the nearer retreating figure. Instantly he was gripped from behind in a vise-like choke hold and the weapon was knocked from his grasp. He rammed his left elbow into his attacker's solar plexus and the grip was released. Pivoting on his left foot, he whirled around to deliver a blow with his right fist. The other man just managed to block it from crashing into his face.

"Damn it, Jude! What's wrong with you?" John exclaimed angrily upon recognizing him. He bent over coughing and rubbing his throat.

"Greetings to you, too, brother," Jude returned with one of his rare, genuine smiles.

He held one hand to his throbbing abdomen and offered his former comrade the other. John clasped it without reservation. In spite of the pain, he, too, was sincerely glad to meet again after the intervening time.

John retrieved his gun from the pavement and concealed it once more. They were at the farthest end of the parking lot. Behind the cars parked at this extreme was a low wall. The two men leaned against it and talked.

"Okay, Jude. I'm here because of your phone call earlier today. Of course, you planned for me to come to see and hear what I did. Now, why did you stop me?"

"These men are my brothers, also. They trust me as their leader and honor me by obeying what I command. I protect my own; therefore, I could not let you kill them.

But, likewise, I could not leave you ignorant of what threatens Nathan Perry."

"And how do you know that I won't turn you in to the police?"

Jude gave a short, scornful laugh. "Even if you were to do so, you know my opinion of those 'civil servants.' My arrest would be of little concern to me. And I would not betray my people to their authority…, no matter how 'persuasive' they became." He casually swiped his forefinger across the scar on his face as proof of this point.

"What do you have against Nathan?"

"Nothing.

"Then why not refuse this hit or at least tell me who contracted for it?" demanded John.

"I have my reasons. They need not concern you at present. Besides, I have always believed that Allah protects true men of destiny whose hearts are pure. He allows them to live until his purposes for them are accomplished. If Congressman Perry is such a man, then he has nothing to fear."

"What right have you or I to judge another man's heart, Jude?"

"It is Allah who judges, John. The balance of life and death is held firmly in *his* hand. May Nathan not be weighed on the scales and found wanting."

"So, it's still like that with you? All right then, so let it be," John said resignedly. "Our business here tonight is finished. I have to get back." He looked straight into Jude's face and spoke. "I would deeply regret having to sacrifice one friend to save another, but, like you, *I will* protect what has been committed to *me*. You do understand, don't you?"

"We have always understood one another."

Once again, they parted as they had grown accustomed to doing ever since the first time that Jude had smuggled John into one of his organization's "training camps" when they were both students. Each man clasped the other's left hand; each man clenched his own right hand into a fist and placed it over his heart.

"Laa takhaf," Jude said sincerely.

"Laa takhaf," John replied in kind.

They then went their separate ways.

Monday
July 3, 2000
9:00 p.m.

Elsewhere in the river district, there was also notable activity, but of a different sort. The Beauvoir Room at Cypress Vale Mansion Inn was the scene of a private gathering that was now in full swing. The members of the development group known as "the Commission,"

102

along with their significant others, were enjoying their annual American Patriots' Dinner, an affair which for the past five years had been held on the *eve* of the Fourth of July.

The more cynical members of the Vicksburg community had often commented upon the name of this event and the date of its occurrence. It was a well-known fact, they observed, that during the Civil War, the last day of independence for the **Confederate** stronghold of Vicksburg was July 3, 1863. After a siege of the city enduring more than a month, Lieutenant General John C. Pemberton had officially surrendered it to Major General Ulysses S. Grant on the following day, July 4. And though the words *American* and *Patriots'* might put off anyone who protested the date of the dinner, the critics still raised the question: **Which** independence is the Commission choosing to commemorate and thus to celebrate?

At any rate, this year's banquet was particularly festive, and with good reason. The state legislature had just passed a bill which allowed for five years of tax breaks for developers of "environmentally impacted property that meets specific guidelines." This legislation seemed tailor-made for the Heights Project, and, in truth, it was just that. Lobbyists in Jackson had called in a considerable number of favors to get it passed.

The hostess of the gathering, Mrs. Julia Pembroke Leigh, sat regally at the head table. Carlisle Forrest served as Master of Ceremonies and, by virtue of his association with Julia, as unofficial host. He was leading the company in a toast. Although she raised her glass dutifully and smiled graciously, Julia was not fully present in the moment. Ever sensitive to her moods, Carlisle perceived this and the knowledge both concerned and irritated him. He felt that she should be more supportive of him in what he considered to be a personal moment of glory.

After introducing the chairman of their group, he yielded the microphone and lectern to that gentleman and returned to his seat beside Julia. He lightly caressed her shoulder as he sat down as though to call her back from wherever her thoughts had lured her. She turned to him, placed her hand on his and offered an appeasing smile, which, he noted, did not extend to her eyes. The detachment was still there. Carlisle's annoyance increased.

Wade Breckinridge, leader of the Commission, spoke of current and future ventures, of profits already accrued and of those projected. He mentioned Demeter in tones of great satisfaction and high expectation, and praised Carlisle for his successful efforts in attracting new commercial and industrial tenants to the complex. He then turned his comments to the Heights Project and applauded the boon that they had received from the Mississippi legislature. Mr. Breckinridge expressed his confidence that the favorable climate for "visionary entrepreneurship" would continue and even improve in the near future. "Because," he assured, "I have faith that the *right* person will accede to the Oval Office, having risen above the field of contenders."

At these words Julia, remembering their conversation just three days ago, glanced furtively at Carlisle. He seemed fully attuned to the speech. But did she detect a silent communication—a quick glance, a slight nod of confirmation—between him and the speaker? Or did she only imagine it?

To ease the mental strain, she allowed her gaze to glide across her favorite of the private meeting rooms.

Clustered about the dais, circular tables clothed in white linen accommodated the dining of notable personages with china, silverware, and crystal befitting the occasion. Her eyes skimmed over these to the sycamore wainscoting and followed this fine-textured hardwood as it ascended to frame three panels on each of the side walls and climbed even further to form the crown molding. Each panel was adorned with a damasked silk wall covering, providing a rich backdrop for the painting of a magnolia blossom. Suspended in splendor from a ceiling medallion was a glittering chandelier. Her vision dutifully captured the splendor for her brain, yet its pleasure receptors remained ignored. Carlisle and the Commission were not the only sources of her unrest. Something else, a letter—a voice from the past, from the grave and beyond—had also arrested her mind's focus and even now threw her thoughts into turmoil.

"If I am going to do anything about all of this—and, God help me, I must—I have to act now."

Breckinridge's speech had concluded and applause clattered loudly about the room. Julia excused herself, telling Carlisle that she was going to the powder room. Rushing down the main hall to the Master's Drawing Room, she slipped through the double doors. She did not want bright light seen from beneath the portals to signal that the room was occupied, so she bypassed the switch for the main lighting. She maneuvered deftly in the darkness, familiarity making her steps sure. Gaining the desk, she switched on a discreet reading lamp, pulled open one of the deep bottom drawers, and took out a telephone directory. Casting apprehensive looks at the double doors as she proceeded, she flipped rapidly to the

P's. "Perrin . . . Perrit . . . Perry. Here it is. 'O. Perry' on Warrenton Road." She jabbed the keys of the appropriate numbers, heard the ring tone, heard the click at the other end of the line.

"Hello. This is the Perry residence. How may I help you?" Olivia asked.

Monday
July 3, 2000
10:00 p.m.

"I'm afraid that his arm is broken, sir," said the young emergency room physician. "No other broken bones. He's suffered a mild concussion; that's why he was unconscious for a while. He'll have a bruised forehead and his head will hurt for a few days. Strangely enough, seeing that he fell while the swing was in the air, there are no lacerations, no abrasions— no ruptures of the skin at all. No bleeding externally or internally. It's almost uncanny. He's a lucky boy."

Nathan remembered the wave of relief he had felt at the doctor's words. He now stood over the bed of his sleeping child watching his wife tenderly kiss the boy's cheek. He closed his eyes, and the images of the evening's harrowing events replayed themselves on the screen of his mind: Richard lying face down in the rough white gravel, his arm bent under his body from where he had extended it to try to break the fall; tearing down I-20 West at killer speed in the back seat of Scott Kendricks's jeep; cradling his son's small, limp body in his arms; having to tell Richard's mother.

Damaris had arrived at the hospital later. He had delayed calling her until he knew the full extent of Richard's injuries. She had rushed into the emergency room silent and strained, her fingers interlocking, her hands clasped tightly together as she willed herself to remain reasonably calm. Nathan had dreaded facing her, dreaded having to bear her look of blame. Before any words were spoken, he had searched her face quickly. Her eyes had shown questioning alarm but no accusation, and he silently thanked her.

But now he wanted to be alone with his son. Yet he dared not make the request of Damaris. Her maternal sensibilities had been shocked enough today. The understanding and temperance she had displayed earlier were not inexhaustible, nor did they override her concern for and proctectiveness of her child. He knew this and kept silent.

His wife, however, through some newly heightened intuition, sensed his need. She rose from beside Richard's bed.

"Nathan, I'm exhausted. Are you coming to bed now?"

"No, not yet. I thought I'd stay with him a bit longer."

"All right, then. I'll tell Mrs. DuBois to wait. She asked if she could sit with him tonight to make sure that he rests comfortably. This incident has really shaken her.

She even asked if she could come now and perform a ritual to invoke a 'protector spirit', as she called it, on Richard's behalf."

"No!" Nathan exclaimed. "Keep her out of here with that!" His reaction was so visceral, so violent that it surprised both him and his wife.

"*Calm down*, Nathan. Of course I strictly forbade her to do it. She's known from the beginning of her time with us that such actions would cost her this job. I overlooked the matter this time only because I knew she acted out of genuine concern for Richie. I'm touched that she would be willing to revert to her old Voodoo ways and risk being fired in order to try to protect him."

She looked as him more closely. "Are you certain that you're all right?"

"Yes," he said, somewhat subdued. "I'm sorry that I overreacted. I guess I'm more stressed than I realized."

"I understand," she said softly. "You're allowed to be human, Sundiata. And it's fine with me if you want to stay in here with our baby tonight. I'll tell Mrs. Dubois that he's in good hands."

She turned toward the door connecting their suite to their son's room but his hand upon her arm detained her.

"Damaris, wait a minute. I just want to say that I'm *truly sorry* that I let this happen to Richie. I should have—" Her forefinger pressed gently against his lips stopped the words.

"Sh-h! Don't talk like that. You didn't *let* this happen, Nathan. It was an accident. You are Richard's father; no other man loves him more. I <u>trust</u> <u>you</u> with our son's life, and I hope that you trust me the same." She touched her palm to his cheek. "Okay?"

He gently took her hand in his. "Okay," he said tenderly. Then she left the room. Something had changed about her, he decided, but right now he did not try to ponder it. The other thing pressed too hard upon him.

Nathan wearily flung himself in the armchair beside the bed. His clothes looked as though he had slept in them. His countenance was strained. Removing his glasses, he slowly rubbed his hand back and forth across his brow. His mind flashed back to the questions he had asked Richard as they rode from the hospital back to the bed and breakfast.

"Richard, why did you jump from the swing while you were so high up, son?"
"The voice," Richard said simply.
"What voice?" Nathan asked.
"See, Daddy, I was swinging and looking at those woods across the fence. I closed my eyes and pretended that I was flying high above them, high above the tallest trees. The sunshine felt good against my face. Then the voice said, 'Jump and you'll <u>really</u> fly!' So, I jumped."
"What did this 'voice' sound like, Richard?"
"It sounded like <u>you</u>, Dad. That's why I jumped."
The words sent a chill through Nathan.
"No, son," he said solemnly, "it wasn't me."

He now reached into his pants pocket and pulled out two folded strips of paper. Scott had given them to him just before the minister had left the Perrys at the hospital.

"Call me if I can do anything more to help," he had said before driving off.

He unfolded the two pieces of paper. Scribbled on one were Scott's home and office phone numbers. A scripture reference was written on the other: Proverbs 26:1-2. Nathan stared at the second strip of paper for several minutes. Then, resignedly, he put his glasses back on and pulled open the drawer of the nightstand between the armchair and Richard's bedside. He took out the Gideon Bible which he, a seasoned traveler, was assured of finding. He was also accustomed to ignoring it. But not tonight. No, not tonight.

Monday
July 3, 2000
11:00 p.m.

"Mr. Johnston, you will be stationed at one end of the stage. Mr. Stuart, you will be positioned at the other."

Ultimately, John did not fully trust the Secret Service officers assigned to Nathan. When placing security closest to the primaries in this political campaign, he turned first to the two men that he had handpicked. He had met David Johnston and Michael Stuart at his gym. The human resources department at his firm had run special background checks on them. John, after reviewing their findings, had immediately recruited both as bodyguards for the Perry presidential campaign.

Some viewed this as a high-risk move, since both men were ex-convicts. However, John had reasoned thus:

"Any person who can endure prison and keep his mind and his manhood intact and can then go on to rebuild his life is strong enough mentally and physically to protect my people." This rationale combined with his tendency to empathize with those who had clashed with the law and survived.

"At both ends of the stage, a police officer will be standing at the base of the steps leading from the ground up to the platform. Officers will also be deployed within the crowd and along the perimeter of the court house grounds, as will be the Secret Service personnel. You two will be wired and able to communicate with the police and with me. From your elevated vantage point, you will both have a better view of the crowd. If you see anyone or anything suspicious, notify the police first and then me. Hopefully, any threat that arises can be neutralized with minimal disruption. Use deadly force only as a last resort; we want to avoid endangering innocent bystanders."

"Where will you be, Mr. Henderson?" asked Johnston, his hazel eyes held a look of concerned inquiry.

"Wherever I can do the most to help maintain security," John replied. "Are there any other questions, gentlemen? All right then. Get a good night's rest. We'll all need to be at 100 percent on tomorrow."

After dismissing Johnston and Stuart from their meeting in the Linden Plantation's great room, John retired to his suite. Antoinette awaited him in the sitting room. She greeted him with a kiss then took his hand and led him to the sofa. He really did not feel like talking but knew that she wanted to and thus yielded.

"What's going on John?" she asked directly.

"What do you mean, sweetheart?" he returned.

"You've been gone from seven o'clock until now. And nobody knew where you were."

"I told you earlier, Antoinette, I had business to handle."

"Have you heard about Richard?

"Heard what? What's happened to him?" John asked quickly, genuinely concerned.

"He had an accident out at Scott's place. He fell and broke his arm," Antoinette said.

"What! How is he doing now? Is he here or at the hospital?"

"He's here. I spoke with Damaris earlier tonight, and she said that he's intrigued with his cast and wants everyone to sign it. He's going to be fine."

"I'm glad to hear that. He's a sharp little man. I'll check in on him tomorrow."

"So, what was this business that you had to attend to?" asked Antoinette, undeterred.

"Security business for Nathan's speech at the court house," he replied, purposely sounding nonchalant.

"Oh? You're adding to the guard on him? Why? Is there a problem?"

"I got a tip that someone may try to cause a disturbance. I told Nathan, but he wouldn't cancel. So, I decided to take a few extra precautions; that's all. Now, enough about campaign matters. I'm through with work for tonight."

She was about to protest, but thought better of it.

"Whe-e-e-w," he emitted a long, low whistle of delight after taking time to really look at her. Girl, you are gorgeous. Is that a new negligee?"

"Yes. I bought it today. I'm glad that you like it."

"I do like it," he held a sheer, shimmering sleeve between his fingers. "It's exquisite, but even more so because it adorns the beautiful woman that I love."

His compliment was sincere, but he also sought to make up for the half truths he had just told her.

"Before I get any closer to you, I need to grab a shower, Ann. Keep the bed warm for me."

Antoinette heard the steady pattering of the water against the shower stall. She knew that John was not telling her everything, for she had a deep sense of foreboding. She walked over to the bed, knelt at the side where he usually slept and began to pray.

Some minutes later, she was still there, caught up. She did not hear the bathroom door open, did not know that her husband stood there in his bathrobe, respectfully silent. He found himself listening and heard his name called out. He could not help bowing his head in the presence of such reverence and of such fervent supplication.

Then, she was finished. He remained unseen, for her back was turned toward him. John saw her take two tissues from the box on the nightstand and dab at her eyes. Without turning around, she rose, went around to her side of the bed and lay down. He reached and shut the door audibly as though he had just emerged from the bathroom.

Hearing the door close, Antoinette, now smiling serenely, turned to face him. He lay down beside her, took her in his arms, and just held her close, as though he pressed a precious treasure to his heart.

Monday
July 3, 2000
11:30 p.m.

'"As snow in summer, and as rain in harvest, so honor is not seemly for a fool. As the bird by wandering, as the swallow by flying, so the curse causeless shall not come.'

So I'm a cursed fool? Is that what I am to believe?" Nathan indignantly asked over the telephone. He'd made use of Scott's number.

"The verses are simply making comparisons. Snow in summer, rain at harvest time, honoring a fool, and a curse without a cause—all are unnatural or abnormal," Scott returned patiently.

"Look, I don' t know what to do. I thought that I had lost my son out there today. I was afraid that he had broken his neck!"

"But you *didn't* lose him because he *didn't* break his neck. Be thankful, man. God knows that you want to protect Richard and keep him safe."

"*How?* How do I do that? How do I stop this—this thing—whatever it is—that's taking out the male line of my family?"

"Are you a righteous man, Nathan?"

"What? What are you talking about?"

"Do you walk uprightly? Do you speak the truth from your heart? Are you without deceit?"

For several moments the other end of the line was silent. "No," came the terse reply.

"Then you've opened the door to allow a curse to operate in your life."

"Oh, I see. Now, of course, you're going to tell me that 'Jesus can make it right.'"

"Better than that. He can make *you* right."

"My mother and I, we—well, _I_—gave up on him when my father died."

"Thankfully, _He_ did not give up on _you_ at that time. He has too much invested; He bought you with his blood when He was crucified. That's powerful enough to redeem your life and to annihilate any curse upon it."

"Why is blood required?" demanded Nathan.

"Sin causes a curse. Take care of the sin and you also take care of the curse. It takes pure blood to pay the price for sin and to free a life from the death sentence that sin brings."

"Wait a minute, this thing in my family began years ago. It didn't just start with me."

"But it can end with you. The blood of Jesus Christ washes away the sin of all who confess Him and believe in Him. If there are consequences of sin that a believer must face, the Lord will grace him to deal with them. But, his _debt_ is paid in full. The blood of Jesus is the only currency that God will accept for the sin debt. It is the only thing that makes you guiltless in His sight."

"All this from a mixed-blood Jew nailed to a white man's cross and used for years to keep the black man subjugated?" Nathan spat out the words. "You expect me to _accept_ that?"

Scott's temper flared at this irreverence. The influence of John Henderson was indeed strong. Scott knew the power of the words, for he had once ardently believed them himself.

"*All this* from Jesus Christ, the only begotten Son of God with the blood of God! No man's sperm had anything to do with it. His blood was divine and pure, free from the taint of Adam's sin. *That* came from His Father. His race was Semitic. He was an Israelite, a Jew from the tribe of Judah. *That* came from His mother.

And before you try to dismiss him as being "mixed," you better realize that blackness was in His mix. Two of the sources thereof were Rahab and Bathsheba, black women who became Jews by submitting to the God of their husbands. Your own wife acted similarly when she adopted the faith of her Jewish father. So, aren't *you* married to a "mixed-blood Jew"?

"Yes! And *you* are well aware of that, aren't you, preacher? I've seen the way that you look at her. I saw it from the first time that you met her! Tell me, does your Jesus allow you to low-rate *me* when all this time *you've* had a hard on for my wife?"

The pang of conviction caused a split second's hesitation. But Scott fought against the condemnation that threatened to follow and silence his words.

"I'm a man just like you are; I appreciate a woman's beauty. Looking isn't always lusting. *Your* concern should be whether *you're* giving your wife what she needs to keep her from looking twice at me or any other man. What about it, Nathan? Is the fountain flowing at your house, or is Damaris drying up with thirst?

"Shut up, Scott!" It was the minister's turn to strike a nerve. His meaning was all too clear.

Scott could sense Nathan struggling to control his anger before he spoke in tense, deliberate words.

"Christianity is _not_ a religion for black men. You, me, John—that's what we all once believed and got others to believe. _You're_ the one who sold out."

"This is not about a religion; it's about a relationship. It's offered to every man, regardless of his color. I didn't 'sell out'; I surrendered—to the power of God."

"I've turned my back on all of that for so long. It's too damned late!"

"As long as you are still breathing, it is not too late. _Now_ is the time of salvation. _Now_ is _your_ time, Nathan. What will you do?"

****

Midnight

The wall clock in the bedroom was shaped like a sunburst. Intricately graven red-gold metal radiated from the time-keeping disc. Ticking, measured and precise, was amplified by the quietness of the room. Like a beating heart, the sound was strong and sure, a testimony to the force of life. Then, in synchronized exactness, the minute and hour hands aligned themselves on "XII". The clock obediently chimed out the hour. Downstairs the grandfather clock lent its baritone tolling to the tenor of the chimes. The combined sound drowned out the ticking, as though interrupting the force of life and summoning souls to judgment. The sole listener was sharply affected. She counted the twelve strokes. Were the clocks also tolling out the remaining hours, the minutes, the seconds of her son's life? Her mind railed against the thought.

Her earlier plans of being in bed by 10:00 p.m. for some much needed rest had long before been smashed by an urgent and incredible telephone call. Now, as was her custom when faced with overwhelming circumstances, Olivia paced to and fro, speaking her mind out loud. Her audible voice lent tangibility to her thoughts and brought them more under her control. And she *must* keep control.

"It's here. It's his birthday. Lord help us. All right, all right. I called the police and found that John had already alerted them about the threat of an assassination. They said that they had tried to bring in a suspect whose name John had given them, but the man had eluded them. Okay. When I talked to John, he said that Nathan wouldn't call off his speech. Of course not! I knew that he wouldn't; I *knew* it! He's his father's son. Life is cheap when compared with their causes. God! Why? Why did I stupidly become the wife of one death-hungry martyr and the mother of another? I won't risk trying to dissuade Nathan; at this point I don't trust myself not to become hysterical with him. I can't afford to do that; I must keep myself together so that I can think. Think, Olivia. F-o-c-u-s. All right. Now, that woman who called me refused to name names, but she was certain that an attempt would be made against Nathan's life. I'm sure that she was Julia Leigh, but I have no proof of it. She has too much clout for the police to question her without evidence.

"Damn her! *All* she had to do was to say who's behind this. And what did she mean about ' knowing the truth about Nathan'? I could drive up to that hotel of hers right now and beat the sh—the information out of her. No, Olivia, no. You'd be arrested, and you can't help your child from a jail cell. You need to get a grip on yourself. Okay. Let me see. I must talk to Julia Leigh, and I must do it calmly and rationally in order to learn what I must know. This I will do for Nathan and for Richard [she remembered her own fear when Nathan had told her of his disturbing accident]. She *will* tell me the truth, and may God have mercy on both of us, for I have none for her."

She stopped in the middle of the room and looked at the clock. "It's 12:30; I'd better try to get some sleep."

Before lying down she knew that there was one more thing that she had to do.

Right after Ellis's death, she had distanced herself from her God. She had felt hurt, cheated, and forsaken. But she could not totally reject her faith as Nathan had; it had become too much a part of her. Instead, she had retreated into unyielding self-reliance: "*So, that's the way it is. I can't depend on God to come through for me when it really matters. Then I won't ask Him to or expect Him to. He's God; He does what He wants. That's His right. So, I'll make certain that I take care of myself and that I take care of my son until he's grown and on his own.*" Olivia would have denied having ever spoken or having thought these words after her husband died. But her actions had spoken them. As the years passed, however, she had prospered and had also matured and increased her understanding of life. Many times over, she had seen what she had grudgingly acknowledged as a divine hand operating on behalf of her and her son, gracing them with favor. Now, twenty-four years after she had become a widow, the rift between her and her God had narrowed to a small fissure within her heart, one not incapable of being healed.

She knelt beside her bed and prayed, saying simply, "God, You already know the end of all of this. I ask You, please, to protect my son. If there is something that has been done to bring this upon our family, Lord God, I humbly ask You to let *me* know it and show *me* how to correct it. I can't stand this helplessness! Show me, please, for Nathan's sake and for Richard's. . . . but even so, not my will, but Yours be done. In the name of Jesus Christ, I pray. Amen."

****

The Sixth Day
(*Mayhem, Murders and
Matriarchs*)

Tuesday
July 4, 2000
4:00 a.m.

*"In Old Testament times, God ordered the Israelites to
establish six cities of refuge," Scott said. "These cities were
to shelter individuals who had accidentally killed people until
they could stand before the congregation in judgment. As
long as these individuals remained within the walls of the
refuge cities, those who sought to retaliate against them were
forbidden to do so. However, if the refugees left the cities,
they were fair game for the 'revengers' of blood," the minister
proclaimed.*

*"In the New Testament, Jesus Christ is our City of Refuge.
As long as we remain in Him, God will not extract from us the
penalty for the sin debt incurred by Adam, the natural father
of mankind. The penalty for that debt is death.*

*"The Old Testament refugees had slain others and had
polluted the land with their blood. In the judgment, if it was
found that they had acted out of enmity with intent to kill,
then the penalty was death, for God said, ' ... ye shall not
pollute the land wherein ye are: **for blood it defileth the
land: and the land cannot be cleansed of the blood that
is shed therein, but by the blood of him that shed it.***'*

*"Similarly, when we stand in the judgment before Christ,
we will have no need to fear, for He paid the debt of sin with
His blood, and He suffered the penalty for sin with His death.
Blessed be His name forever and ever! Amen.*

With startling calm, Olivia decided that she was
either dreaming or having a nervous breakdown. Her
eyes were open and she was conscious. She could *see*
herself sitting in one of the pews in the sanctuary of
Apostles' Creed as she had actually done two days ago.

How strange! At the time, she had only half listened to Scott's sermon, her mind being filled with her own pressing concerns. But now, she *saw* herself sitting there, hanging on every word. What's more, every spoken syllable was now resounding in her conscious mind. How could it replay what she didn't remember ever having heard? Was this what a vision was like?

When she was fully awake, she could say almost verbatim the words that had been emphasized: "… and the land cannot be cleansed of the blood that is shed therein, but by the blood of him that shed it."

Tuesday
July 4, 2000
9:00 a.m.

The American Patriots' Dinner had extended into the wee hours of the morning. Carlisle Forrest had earlier reserved the suite adjoining Julia's, having anticipated the gala's late ending and his unwillingness/unfitness (thanks to generous alcoholic refreshment) to drive home afterwards. He and she were enjoying breakfast in the living room of her suite.

"These eggs and sausages are delicious."

"Well, of course they are. I ordered room service to bring up our special 'country breakfast' just for you. Here at Cypress Vale Mansion Inn, sir, we strive to please," Julia replied with a glowing smile.

"And *you* *do* *please* extremely well," Carlisle returned meaningfully, "if I remember correctly."

"So, what are your plans for today?"

"Well, of course, I've closed my offices for the Fourth. Not many people are in the mood for buying property today. They'll be too busy eating, drinking, playing, and partying to excess, all in the name of liberty. Tomorrow will find them less patriotic and more practical. Then the Forrest Realty Company will welcome them and their wallets with open arms."

"So, you're pretty much at your leisure?" She intensely desired to know his movements for this Independence Day, but she did not want to appear anxious.

"Pretty much, . . .except for one brief business matter that I must oversee around noon. Therefore, I'll be well rested and refreshed for the festivities on the river tonight."

"I'm very happy that you're portraying my great grandfather in the re-enactment."

"It's both an honor and a pleasure. I have always greatly admired Julius Pembroke. He and I would have gotten along famously. He understood the importance of empire building and of preserving the *correct* social order. He knew what it meant to start with modest means and to exert his brains, blood, and sweat to realize a dream of wealth and power."

"It's sad that Poppa did not hold him in such high esteem as you do."

"With all due respect to your late father, Julia, James Pembroke was a scholar who acquired commendable skill in *managing* a great estate, not in building it." He paused for a moment and added quietly, "He also was consistent in pointing out that my family were third-generation employees of the Pembrokes, thus rendering me unfit as a suitor for his beloved daughter."

"That never made any difference to me, did it?" she challenged.

"In all honesty, I would have to answer 'yes' and 'no' to that question."

"What do you mean?"

"I mean that I was good enough for you to love, but not good enough for you to marry. Good enough to take to bed but never good enough to meet at the altar." His best efforts could not completely gloss over the old hurt and resentment.

"You're being grossly unfair and you know it!" Julia hotly protested. "Besides, that's all ancient history now. Must we allow it to taint the present?"

"No, definitely not," he said confidently. "The present grows more promising each minute and will develop into a bright future. I'm going to make it happen for us, and you shall see."

Her concern was now quite evident. "Carlisle, please listen. You have *nothing* to prove, to me or to anyone else."

"That's where you're wrong, sweet Julia. I do, and I will."

Tuesday
July 4, 2000
11:00 a.m.

Resting atop a high terraced hill, the Old Court House Museum encompassed a city block. The base of the hill was fortified by a brick wall with a stone façade. At certain points the wall was nine feet high or more. At the east entrance, a long flight of steps ascended from the ground level at the sidewalk up to the hill's flattened brow. From there a stone walk bisected the lawn and led to a shorter set of steps. Climbing these accessed the portico at the front of the building. Six massive ionic columns supported the portico roof which in turn formed the floor of the second story balcony. Still upward the colonnade soared until their capitals rested directly beneath the entablature under the main roof. The side and rear entrances repeated the grandeur of the front, though somewhat less imposingly.

The museum was a testimony to the stately beauty of classical Greek architecture. One hundred and forty-two years after its construction began as the Warren County Court House, it still stood, a silent witness to the vision of its architects and to the skill of the enslaved Negro artisans who had constructed it.

The four peaked roofs of the building faced east, north, south, and west. At the point where the rear portions of the roofs intersected, a cupola rose crowned with a belfry. On the hour the cupola's huge clock chimed out the time, and the bell doled in resonating agreement. Yet even with this regular and solemn marking of time, there was a timelessness about this place. It conjured up images of bygone days in a realm known as the "Old South" where palatial mansions, vast cultivated fields, and privileged white "nobility" existed in sharp contrast to tottering shacks, back-breaking field labor, and blacks held in slavery. The mind could also envision with clarity the other social classes which fell between these two extremes.

Then had come the conflagration historically dubbed the Civil War, but known by many white Southerners as "The War Between the States." For, indeed, to them it had been a conflict involving two sets of states, two ideologies, two nations. Bitter had been their fight; more bitter still their defeat. Perhaps that was why a haunting spirit of despair and defiance brooded over the building. Surely, the ghosts of long-dead Confederate soldiers glided restlessly over its grounds, peered out through windows of unused rooms, lingered possessively over displayed artifacts of "The War."

Cherry Street on the east, Jackson Street on the north, Grove Street on the south, and Monroe Street on the west—in one hour all four thoroughfares framing the Old Court House Museum would teem with people. The majority would be African Americans, but substantial numbers of Asian Americans, European Americans, Latin Americans, and Native Americans would make themselves known. Nathan Perry had amassed so

127

diversified a following. Loudspeakers had been affixed to all four sides of the building. Perry would deliver his speech from the east side of the edifice. A platform draped with red, white, and blue banners had already been erected in front of the portico. Coveted reserved chairs had been neatly arranged on the uppermost terrace of the front lawn. On the building's west side, a giant television screen reared itself from the bricked pavement, waiting to project a simultaneous video image of the live event as it unfolded.

How would he address such a crowd, at such a place, on such a day as this? Would his words silence the stubborn echoes of the past? Would they address the outspoken demands of the present? *Could* they shape the future?

Tuesday
July 4, 2000
11:30 a.m.

Each street that surrounded the Old Court House Museum was cordoned off to motor vehicles as far as two blocks from the building. People had begun to arrive on foot as early as 9:30 a.m. Congressman Perry's immediate family members, friends, acquaintances, and campaign associates were, of course, in attendance. Both Nathan and John had been unsuccessful in convincing their spouses not to come. They had, however, been handicapped in their persuasion, not wanting to fully disclose the danger and risk alarming them. But somehow both women sensed the threat, and therefore, each one wanted to be with her husband even more.

Thus Damaris Perry and Antoinette Henderson had made an unspoken pact with their mates: "We will not pressure you to confirm the truth that we already know if you will allow us to come with you."

No one had dared to suggest to Olivia that she should stay away for her own safety's sake. When the Perry motorcade had stopped at her house, Nathan had attempted to bring up the matter before he escorted his mother to the waiting limousine. But she had leveled a look of such fierce resolution at him that he had respectfully yielded.

Pastor Scott Kendricks was to give the invocation at John Henderson's special request. Congresswoman Cecilia Sherman was slated to introduce the speaker. As an added precaution, Richard would not sit with his parents and grandmother on the stage but would be seated in the reserved section with the vigilant Mrs. Dubois. A secret service agent would be stationed at each end of the row on which they sat. Thus, all was in readiness.

Tuesday
July 4, 2000
Noon

If every person assembled at or near the Old Court House Museum that day had represented a vote for Nathan Sundiata Perry in the upcoming Presidential Election, then the Freedom Party could easily have had Mississippi in its pocket. Thousands waited to hear him speak. And so after Cecilia's brief introduction, he began.

"The face of America is black; the face of America is brown; the face of America is red; the face of America is white; the face of America is yellow. The United States is no longer a nation *with* minorities. It is a nation *of* minorities. But together we make up a unique majority, the *American* majority. E pluribus unum: 'Out of many, one.' That motto is inscribed on the official seal of our country. We are united by our ardent belief in and our unshakeable commitment to ideals set forth on another July 4 that dawned 124 years ago in the great state of Pennsylvania, which I have been honored to represent in the United States Congress. On that day, in the city of Philadelphia, the Declaration of Independence was signed. It began with these revolutionary words: 'We hold these truths to be self-evident, that all men are created equal.' That, ladies and gentlemen, means equal access to all that our great country has made available through the hard labor, cutting edge ingenuity, and awesome creativity of its people. That means *equal* access to good jobs, *equal* access to quality education, *equal* access to excellent healthcare. . ."

(Many a Perry supporter standing afar off in the crowds may have envied the close-up view of one particular spectator. With crystal clarity he saw Nathan's face above the lectern—for he peered at it through the crosshairs in the scope of a Soviet SVD Dragunov rifle.)

"… We believe that life, liberty, and the pursuit of happiness are our God-given rights, and we must stand strong against the enemies of freedom, both domestic and foreign, who want to take them from us. To do this, we will better equip our police forces and have officers, in vehicles and on foot, patrolling high crime areas. We will attack the poverty and hopelessness that feed crime in these neighborhoods. Let us force absentee landlords to clean up, fix up, or else tear down and remove the decaying hulks in which residents are forced to live. Let us fund academic and vocational/ technical programs for underprivileged youth that they may one day know the pride of being productive, taxpaying citizens of a free nation.

Let us punish to the full extent of the law those leeches who prey on the trustfulness of the consumer, on the desperation of the poor, on the vulnerability of the elderly and the infirm, and on the innocence of children, whether they are child molesters in dark alleys or corporate thieves in high-rise penthouses.

"We will also strengthen our military and empower our fighting men and women with the best training, the best technology, and the best moral support from the home front. Our wounded soldiers will be celebrated and cared for with state of the art medical attention. How dare we do less for those who have risked their lives to keep America secure and free? ..."

(The spectator with the rifle placed a finger on the trigger.)

Seated between Damaris and Scott on the platform, Antoinette whispered to the minister.

"There's something unusual about Nathan's speech today. I can't quite yet decide what it is, but it is definitely different."

"Well, Antoinette, you would be a better judge of that than I would. You've heard more of his speeches." But mentally Scot gave a much less evasive answer, *"Perhaps now he means everything that he says."*

"… But we must work together to live in the reality of that for which the signers of the Declaration of Independence pledged their lives, their fortunes, and their sacred honor. We must put aside selfishness and prejudice. We must be united in upholding the core beliefs and values on which our country was founded. Centuries before Abraham Lincoln gave this warning in the turbulent days preceding the Civil War, [Here he paused for a microsecond to strengthen his resolve to proceed] *Jesus, the Christ* asserted that a house divided against itself cannot stand … ."

Antoinette's eyes widened. "Scott! Did you hear that? Did *I* hear it correctly?" she rasped in disbelief. "Nathan has no use for Christianity. He's been anti-Christian for as long as I've known him. He's never made a reference to the Lord Jesus in any of his speeches."

Scott only smiled at her.

At this point, Nathan turned to his immediate left and beckoned the person seated there to the lectern.

"… So, in the spirit of unity, I want to announce that my esteemed colleague, Congresswoman Cecilia Fairchild Sherman, is now my running mate.

(The finger pressed the trigger.)

Simultaneously, a seismic blast of sound rocked the old court house and ripped through the hot July air as thousands of human voices unleashed shock, outrage, exultation, dismay—whatever emotions were triggered by the prospect of a Perry-Sherman presidential ticket.

The tumultuous noise engulfed the sound of shots, but could not conceal the bright red spot that burst into view on Cecilia's blouse just as Nathan was yielding the microphone to her so that she could address the crowd in her newly publicized role. She reeled backward suddenly and fell. Chaos erupted.

Security personnel and the media sprang into action. Johnston whisked Nathan and Damaris from the stage while Stuart commandeered the removal of Olivia and Antoinette. In them, John had chosen well.

Scott rushed to where Secret Service agents were placing Cecilia Sherman's limp form on a makeshift stretcher to see if he could be of assistance. Sirens blared in the background as a multitude of reporters' cameras flashed like lightning.

Policemen with guns drawn threaded the panicked masses and strove to clear them from the east lawn of the old court house. The agent charged with the safety of Richard Perry and Mrs. Dubois had swiftly conducted them to a waiting staff vehicle which had spirited them away. All were accounted for—except for one person.

On the east roof of the Old Capitol Museum, a sniper lay dead. His intended target had escaped unscathed. The aim of the would-be assassin had been distorted by a bullet piercing his own skull as he pressed the trigger. John Henderson had *not* missed *his* target. But he had forgotten one thing: Jude always sent his men out in pairs. Thus, he, also, lay on the roof, bleeding. Pain seared like fire through his guts. He had seen the second man too late.

His hands pressed into the ruptured mess of his abdomen, futilely trying to keep inside what the deadly projectiles had ripped out. Before consciousness faded, his thoughts were of his wife and her prayer for him.

And the ghosts in gray marveled at the carnage that men of color wreaked upon one another.

Tuesday
July 4, 2000
6:00 p.m.

"Tragedy marred the Nathan Perry rally in Vicksburg, Mississippi, today as an assassination attempt left two dead and two critically injured. Before an electrified crowd of thousands, Freedom Party Presidential Candidate Nathan Perry delivered a compelling speech of unity and change. In the middle of his oration, he announced that Congresswoman Cecilia Sherman—like Perry, a native Mississippian and his staunch rival in the primaries—would be his running mate in the November Presidential Election, thus confirming the hopes *and* fears of many in both camps. Then, suddenly, the assailant's bullet. . . ."

The voice of the news reporter faded in and out of her conscious thought. She saw the images of the Old Court House Museum on the screen, but they did not register. Their frantic departure from the scene,the frenzied movement of spectators and lawmen, the limousine plowing through the crowd and later speeding east on I-20 with police escort, the grim scene at Jackson's University Medical Center—all were a blur that she had to sweep aside. Her mind, her will, her emotions were bent in one direction.

She finished placing selected items into her purse. Her hand hesitated, hovered briefly over one object, then gripped it firmly and put it into the handbag also. Heading for the front door, she heard the tail end of the news broadcast.

"... a Perry campaign spokesperson said that the Congressman *will* attend Vicksburg's Fourth of July River Festival this evening as planned. The mayor of Vicksburg and the chief of police have guaranteed city law enforcement's full cooperation with the Secret Service and other federal security personnel to insure that ...."

She clicked off the television, exited the house, walked determinedly to her Fifth Avenue and slid in behind the wheel. Her destination: Cypress Vale Mansion Inn.

Tuesday
July 4, 2000
6:30 p.m.

Carlisle was awed at the sight before him. The base of the glass showcase was covered with deep purple velvet. Resting upon it was a Confederate officer's dress uniform painstakingly restored to its original splendor. The gold epaulets and braid accentuated the richness of the soft, dusky gray material. A gleaming sheathed saber lay on one side of the uniform; a pair of immaculate

135

white gloves lay on the other. Encircling the waist was a brilliant gold sash fringed at the ends. Directly above the collar, a plumed hat crowned the display; directly beneath the pants, a holstered ivory-handled Colt Walker guarded it. Numerous pinpoints of light embedded in the glass case bathed the ensemble in a warm glow. No priceless museum piece could have been exhibited more royally.

He and Julia were in the Master's Drawing Room— or, rather, they were and they were not. Pressure on a button in the south wall caused a part of the built-in bookcase to open inward like a door, revealing the shrine-like chamber where they now stood. This was a special feature of the room known only to Julia... until today.

"So, this is the real thing?" he asked.

"It is," she replied.

"He actually wore this?"

"He did, and you will wear it tonight in the re-enactment. My great grandfather would have been honored for you to do so, Carlisle."

"The honor is truly mine, Julia."

Even though a formal dress uniform might be considered inappropriate for a battle scene, she had felt compelled to make this gesture. She wanted to show her esteem for him and she wanted to soothe his angry frustration of which she'd been aware since their late lunch together. His demeanor had contrasted sharply

with the buoyancy of that morning. Julia dared not ask
what had provoked his change in mood because she
already knew. She did not want the words spoken aloud,
for then her conscience would have no place to hide.

Tuesday
July 4, 2000
7:00 p.m.

The Fourth of July River Festival was going full
tilt when the jet black Chrysler Fifth Avenue with its
gleaming silver trim bore down upon the revelers on
Washington Street. Seated in the plush ruby red interior,
the driver drew heavily from her reserves of patience
and self control as she inched her way through the sea
of humanity. Tourists, gamblers, vendors, entertainers,
and security personnel thronged the sidewalks and the
cobblestone pavement. The lure of the river's casinos
challenged the resistance of even the most frugal and
scrupulous celebrants. The preeminent jewel among
these floating gems was the *Sheherazade*, and this
evening she offered the rare attraction of the presence of
a presidential candidate and his lady.

Many happily intoxicated Independence Day patriots
may have questioned their eyes when they saw Union
and Confederate soldiers interspersed throughout the
crowd. Or perhaps they feared that they had somehow
stumbled into a time warp. Of course, more sober
celebrators realized that these "soldiers" were present to
lend authenticity to the evening's upcoming main event,
the re-enactment of a Civil War battle.

The military action that was to be relived had originally occurred between the sailors on the gunboats of Union Rear Admiral David Porter and the soldiers manning South Fort, the Confederate fortification at the south end of Vicksburg.

During the actual battle, a mysterious iron clad vessel had steamed up the river and joined the fight on the side of the Rebels. This nameless gunboat had managed to disable a Yankee vessel before it was caught in the crossfire between the other Union gunboats and the Confederate fort. *It was *assumed* that the rest of Porter's flotilla bombarded and sank it. No one knew for sure. Tonight, more than a century later, the crowds would witness the historic fray from the river banks, from vantage points on Washington Street, from the decks of the casino boats, and from the rear lawn of Cypress Vale. Electric torches had been placed along the river banks to add drama and extra lighting to the scene. Brilliant fireworks displays were scheduled to coincide with the battle. It was to be quite a show, and a current of eager anticipation laced the air.

All of this was wasted upon Olivia as she pressed her way toward her objective. The curving tree-lined front driveway had little chance of impressing her. She knew full well that the Cypress Vale Mansion Inn was owned and operated by the great granddaughter of Julius Pembroke, the man who had been the richest planter and largest slaveholder in pre-Civil War Vicksburg. Indeed, he had possessed her own husband's family. For these reasons, she had purposed never to enter its gates and for the five years of its existence had not done so. Only extreme circumstances could have brought her to its doors.

138

"Good evening. Please tell Mrs. Leigh that Dr. Olivia Perry is here to see her." She spoke in polite, yet authoritative tones to the front desk clerk.

"Yes, ma'am," came the startled reply. Neither Olivia's name nor her views were unknown in Vicksburg. "Is she expecting you?"

"She certainly should be. *Get her* ... please."

The clerk summoned a bellboy, a young Hispanic man in his early twenties, and relayed the request. He moved quickly to comply.

In the interim Olivia glanced about her. In keeping with the historic spirit of the evening, several ladies glided about in antebellum costume, the hems of their elaborate hoop skirts swishing softly against the carpet. She thought of the slaves who had paid the price for such finery back in the days when it was in fashion. She could barely return a civil reply when the women smiled at her and crooned, "Good evening." They, along with practically all of the other guests and staff in the lobby, were making their way to the rear of the inn where the expansive sloping lawn faced the river and offered a bird's eye view of the approaching martial spectacle.

"What am I to expect from Julia Leigh," Olivia thought snidely, *"an incarnation of Scarlet O'Hara from* Gone with the Wind?*"*

But the woman being conducted to her by the bellboy did not fit that description. Her silvery blonde hair was gathered away from her face and held together at the nape of her neck in a loose chignon. She wore a sleeveless, tapered dress of a shimmering mint green satin that stopped just above her ankles. Her jewelry was emeralds with gold trim. Thin-strapped gold sandals with five-inch stiletto heels revealed perfectly pedicured nails. Cool, confident elegance is what she exuded; curt, formal aplomb is what she encountered.

"Dr. Perry? I'm very pleased to make your acquaintance. I've heard a great deal about you."

"Thank you, Mrs. Leigh. *Your* reputation also precedes *you.*"

"Will you come this way? We can converse in the drawing room."

They proceeded down the wide central hallway and soon stood before the double doors bearing the prominent bronze *C* and *V* for handles. Julia swept open the portals, and Olivia Perry stood face-to-face with the full-length portrait of the former master of Cypress Vale Mansion and Cypress Vale Plantation. It stopped her cold. An involuntary gasp shortened her breath and her hand flew instinctively to her heart. Here before her was the Confederate cavalry officer from her nightmare.

"Is something wrong?" asked Julia.

Recovering quickly, Olivia replied, "No, I'm fine …. That is a very impressive painting."

"Thank you," Julia returned proudly as she closed the doors behind them. "That is my great grandfather, Julius Pembroke."

This bit of intelligence struck sharply in Olivia's mind, but she filed it away for the moment.

"Mrs. Leigh, you know why I am here, so I will cut straight to the point. Who is trying to kill my son?"

"Whatever do you mean, Dr. Perry?" Julia's voice sounded strained and unnatural even to her own ears.

"You telephoned my house on Monday and warned that there would be an attempt on his life. That attempt was made today. I ask you again: Who is responsible?"

"Why do you think that I made such a communication to you?"

"The caller i.d. clearly displayed the number of this place. You and I both know that you made the call," Olivia stated tensely. She struggled to restrain herself.

"My establishment is filled to capacity for the holiday. Anyone could have called you that night," Julia countered.

"*How* did you know that the call came at night? I didn't mention that."

"All right! I was the caller. I gave the warning. But your son is alive and unhurt. Be thankful and let it go at that."

The shrill scream of exploding shells pierced the room. Outside the windows overlooking the water, the darkness held a lurid red glow from the artillery fire. Flashes of light briefly

*illuminated the rapt faces of spectators viewing the scene from
Cypress Vale's west lawn. The re-enacted battle on the river
had begun.*

"Are you *insane*? I'll see hell freeze over with both
you and I in it before I 'Let it go at that'!"

Olivia snatched the pistol from her purse and leveled
it at her.

Julia's eyes widened in outrage and fear. "How *dare*
you come here armed! You would shoot me in cold blood
on my own property, like a common street criminal?"

"In less than a heartbeat. Relying on my fists
rather than on Smith and Wesson would give me more
satisfaction, but that might prove to be less effective."
She cocked the weapon. "Tell me who wants Nathan
dead."

"Never," she spat out her refusal.

*A crashing boom from the gunboats' cannon shook the
room.*

The sound was more than sufficient to mask the
sharp report of the pistol. A bullet seared the air within
fractions of an inch of the left side of Julia's face and
buried itself in Julius's image suspended over the
mantelpiece.

Instinctively Julia clasped her cheek then turned
quickly to look at the painting.

"The next one goes through *you*. Now, talk!"

Something snapped. It was as though Olivia, by marring the portrait, had committed the final, blatant desecration of the god-like image that Julia Leigh had held of Julius Pembroke for more than five decades.

Screaming profanities, she lunged for the gun, grasping its barrel.

Piercing the night air with a crescendoing shriek, rockets climbed into the heavens and abruptly terminated in a loud bang. Multicolored sparks rained down from the dark sky. Fireworks now heightened the drama of the mock battle as it escalated to its climax.

Within the drawing room, a real battle raged. The two women violently struggled over the pistol, each desperately bent on turning the lethal barrel away from herself and toward her opponent. Onto the empire desk they crashed, wreaking havoc upon the carefully arranged articles resting on its surface. Each wrestled to get back to her feet without releasing the weapon. Feet, knees, and elbows kicked, jabbed, and stabbed. Legs flailed wildly until they were both upright again. Here Julia's sandals betrayed her as one of the heels slipped on the polished hardwood floor, throwing her off balance. Olivia seized the advantage. Jerking the gun from Julia's grasp with one hand, she delivered a resounding slap across her face with the other. Julia fell to the floor beneath her progenitor's image.

Olivia, breathing heavily in the aftermath of the struggle, stood there, clothes disheveled, hair disarrayed, but with the gun firmly in hand. She looked down at her adversary. Even the powerful impetus of saving her only child could not make her fire a bullet into another living human being without pause. Nevertheless, she aimed and cocked her weapon for the last time.

"Wait, wait," Julia managed to say. Her chest heaved in her effort to catch her breath; she, too, bore the signs of combat. "There's something else you should know. Something more important than the information that you came here for."

"What are you talking about?" Olivia demanded.

"You, me, your son … the Perrys … the Pembrokes . . . my family honor—all these years it's all been a lie!"

Olivia's mind switched into rapid rewind: her shock at seeing the portrait; her vision of the sermon at Apostles' Creed; Scott's certainty about betrayal; Helen's suspicions of blackmail; the fears about the Perry land; her chilling nightmare. It all seemed to begin and end with one person. She lowered the pistol.

"This has something to do with *him*, doesn't it?" she asked, gesturing toward the portrait.

"It has everything to do with him," came the bitter reply.

Julia walked slowly and deliberately to the desk. Seating herself in the desk chair, she unlocked and pulled open the long, narrow center drawer. She removed the false back and detached a folded, yellowed piece of paper taped to the actual back of the drawer.

"Take it," she said resolutely. "It's all there. After you have read it, what you do with your knowledge of its contents is your prerogative."

Olivia took the paper. As she did so, she heard bits and pieces of the conversations of returning spectators as they strolled up the central hallway. They raved over the realness of the "Battle of South Fort," which was what they now called it. Then some particular remarks caught her attention.

"Did you hear about the commotion on the riverboat?"

"Which one?"

"The one with the foreign name that I can never pronounce. Sahara—no, that's not it. Sherara—no, that isn't it either. Hey, help me out here."

"Do you mean the *Scheherazade*?"

"Yes! That's it. Well, a live mortar shell from South Fort almost hit its upper deck."

"What? I didn't think that live ammunition was used in these fake battles. Was anybody hurt?"

"No, but you can bet that they were scared out of their minds. And that's the boat that Nathan Perry was on."

"The brother who's running for president? Man, that's messed up! What if he had been killed? All hell would have broken loose down here in Mississippi."

The voices trailed off as the speakers moved farther away. Olivia looked at Julia who stared back at her but said nothing.

**Tuesday
July 4, 2000
10:00 p.m.**

The soft pulsating of the machines monitoring the vital signs were all that disturbed the quiet of the room. The attending physicians had upgraded the patient's condition from critical to serious but stable. Still he slept. She rose wearily from the chair and walked over to the window. A slight pull on the cord opened the blinds in a downward slant, admitting bands of yellow light from the security lamps arching above the parking lot. Alternating patterns of shadow and light fell at odd angles on the bed and walls.

She had kept vigil since he had come out of surgery. Sometimes she prayed; sometimes she cried; sometimes she raged. Most of the time she was strong in faith; for brief moments she anguished in doubt. The pen and writing paper that she had requested earlier at the nurses' station lay on the seat of the chair. On the paper she had written each part of his name—first, middle, and last. Beside each part she had scribbled scriptures of hope and healing that began with the same letter as the name. These she had recited over and over again during the past six hours.

Memories had flooded her mind from the time that she had arrived at the medical center. Now, she thought of the first time that she had seen him. Even in the midst of this ordeal, her eyes took on a dreamy look as though viewing the scene vividly replayed.

He was walking across the park of Jackson State University on his way to the library. She and one of her sorority sisters were sitting on a bench enjoying the shade of one of the massive oak trees. She checked him out as he approached them. He was tall—at least six feet—and dark. He was plainly clad in gym shoes, jeans, and one of those white, sleeveless spring jerseys that the jocks wore. The color of the shirt made the deep chocolate of his skin richer and darker still. As he drew nearer, the muscles in his arms looked as hard as steel. His hair was low-cut and neatly combed; it seemed soft, like lamb's wool. She longed to feel it against her palm. His stride was quick and purposeful. Passing by them he said, "Good morning, ladies," and beneath his mustache flashed a smile revealing a perfect set of Purex-white teeth. Then and there she mentally vowed, "He will be mine!"

Returning to the present and to her chair, she switched on the floor lamp beside it, picked up the paper and read softly aloud. "John… Alexander…Henderson." Each part of his name was written on a separate line flush with the left margin. Antoinette had drawn one continuous circle around his initials. Read vertically, they spelled *JAH*. "'Sing unto God, sing praises to His name: extol Him that rideth upon the heavens by His name **JAH**, and rejoice before Him,'" she spoke Psalm 68:4 from memory in a voice that faltered with sorrow.

"Thank you, Lord God. You have already marked him with Your great name. Maybe *now*, after all of this, after You have spared his life, maybe *now* he will do as this verse commands."

"Maybe, now, I can," came the strained, whispered reply.

Startled, she looked up and saw him gazing at her, an expression of mingled love and contrition upon his face.

"John!" she exclaimed. She lay herself upon the bed, embracing her husband and sobbing joyfully.

But, in the Critical Care Unit of the hospital, there was no tearful jubilance. The auburn hair was concealed beneath a tight-fitting surgical cap; the green eyes were shut. Two terrified adolescents kept watch as their mother, the potential Vice President of the United States, silently fought for her life.

With an arm encircling the shoulder of each girl, a stout, grandmotherly black woman offered words of comfort. Recently divorced, Cecilia presently had no adult family members at the hospital. Her parents had been vacationing in Greece when they were notified of the shooting, had immediately booked the first available flight back to the States, but still could not get there before midnight. Mrs. Ida M. McClellan, the Sherman family cook and housekeeper, had stepped in to fill the temporary void. Her latest request was that the minister "who had been there for Cecilia when it happened" would come and pray for the congresswoman and her daughters. Scott readily obliged.

Ms. Ida Mae stepped out into the corridor. The bullet that had torn through Cecilia's chest had supposedly been meant for the man who stood there gazing through a window at the scene in her hospital room. He clasped the hand of his wife who stood beside him. The older woman studied Nathan's face. Well aware of the former animosity between them, she had to satisfy herself that he had nothing to do with the shooting of Cecilia. She intended to ask him about it point-blank. Something in his face made her believe that he would tell her the truth.

"Congressman Perry, Mrs. Perry, I've known that girl in there all her life. She didn't deserve this." The elderly lady paused briefly to collect herself and then continued. "I want to be clear about one thing: Was that bullet meant for you, or was *she* the target all along?"

"It was meant for me, ma'am," Nathan said honestly. "And I sorely regret that she was struck by it."

"Well then, it's up to *you* to hunt down all the murdering scum involved in this mess!" she declared emotionally.

"I will, Ms. Ida," Nathan said with quiet resignation.

"Ma'am, you've been here a while, and I know that you'd like to get back to your family for what remains of the holiday. The Congressman and I will look after the girls until their grandparents arrive. Don't worry," Damaris assured her.

Nathan smiled at his wife appreciatively. The two of them were finally in sync. It felt good. Inwardly, his smile deepened as he thought of how he would show his appreciation more intimately later, when they were alone.

"Thank you. You're good people," pronounced Mrs. McClellan. She went back into the hospital room to take her leave of the Sherman girls.

"If Cecilia survives this, I <u>will</u> keep faith with her," Nathan pledged silently. *"And I will keep faith with the American people—**all** of them. May God judge between them and me if I do not."*

"Nathan," Damaris was looking up at him.

"Yes?"

"Happy Birthday, love."

(. . .Therefore if any man be in Christ, he is a new creature: old things are passed away; behold, all things are become new. – 2 Conrinthians 5:17)

****

The Seventh Day   **Wednesday**
(Blood Debts)   **July 5, 2000**
                                    12:01 a.m.

Dearest Adam,

I write this missive to you not as a confession, but as an explanation and a testimony to true manhood. The South's "Glorious Cause" died a decade ago-- and I helped to kill it. I took action to secure your inheritance and to insure that my legacy of honor, wealth, and power encouched in the Pembroke name would endure for generations to come.

Early in 1863, I helped to broker a business deal between the Confederate government and Abraham Dreyfus of New York City, one of the biggest buyers of Pembroke cotton. In exchange for $100,000 in gold, of which the Confederacy was in dire need, Dreyfus, to supply his textile mills, would obtain exclusive rights to all cotton in the southern Mississippi Delta, an area extending from the state's southeastern corner up to Vicksburg. The agreement applied to cotton then available and that produced later in the event of a Southern victory in the War. It was a bargain overwhelmingly favoring Dreyfus, but desperate times called for desperate measures.

In the spring of that year, the gold was to be transported by gunboat up from New Orleans where Dreyfus had banking interests. It was to be secretly unloaded at our family's very own Cypress Landing. Soldiers from the fort at Vicksburg's southern end would receive the gold and return it to the garrison. From there it would be smuggled overland to Atlanta where government officials, overseen by Vice President Alexander Stephens, would disperse it to the Confederate states.

I determined that the gold would become part of the Pembroke fortune. On May 16, 1863, we faced Ulysses S.

Grant at the Battle of Champion's Hill. The cavalry troop that I commanded fought hard and bravely; my saber slashed many Yankee throats that day. Nevertheless, we lost the battle and had to fall back. Our plantation lay in the path of our retreat. I warned Robert Forrest, our overseer, of the Union advance and gave him some vital instructions. I had to rejoin my men, for we were headed back to Vicksburg and the strength of its fortifications.

We re-entered the city on May 17. Once my men were properly installed at the garrison, I obtained permission to ride out to Cypress Vale Mansion, which was down-river from the fort. The gold was to be delivered two days later, and I wanted to make certain that all was in readiness at our dock.

My plan was as follows: I would arrange for trusted men from my troop to be part of the detachment assigned to receive the gold at Cypress Landing. I would secretly tell them where to hide the gold at Cypress Vale in case something went wrong and they had to suddenly abort their mission. Then, of course, I would secretly make sure that something _did_ go wrong.

I would get word to that bastard Grant that a Confederate gunboat would be steaming upriver to help to defend Vicksburg against his upcoming assault. I counted on Grant to have Porter, commander of the Union fleet north of the city, to attack the vessel. Porter would have to steam south to engage the ironclad, meaning that he would have to pass the fort where I was stationed. Fierce fighting would occur as we sought to stop him.

By this time, the crew of the Rebel gunboat, having unloaded its cargo, would have heard the commotion from upriver. The soldiers who had received the gold would have heard the same. _My_ men would think it best to hide the gold and retrieve it when things cooled down, just as I had instructed them to do. The gunboat crew would steam toward the city to assist its defenders. However, from a position on the garrison's south wall commanding artillery fire,* I would "misdirect" the mortars toward the Rebel gunboat and help to sink it. The fewer gold conspirators left alive the better. I would be safer that way.

On May 18, I asked my commanding officer to allow me to go out with the reconnaissance detail, pretending that I needed to get an urgent message to my overseer. The detail was to reconnoiter Grant's encampment that lay between Vicksburg and our plantation. I took with me the slave who had served as my personal attendant in field campaigns for the past two years of war.

When we reached our destination, my slave—his name was Perry—and I quietly separated from the others. I gave Perry the message about the gunboat to take to Grant. I realized that I was taking a chance by writing down the message, but I didn't trust his ability to accurately relay an oral communication. I told him not to return to Vicksburg afterward but to go on home. He did not know, that I had earlier told Forrest that Perry had run away to freedom behind Union lines and that he might try to sneak back and get his woman and their two girls. Yes, I know that this was a lie, but it was a necessary and useful lie. Accordingly, I had told the overseer to kill him on sight if he showed up on the plantation. After leaving the Yankee camp, my slave continued eastward to Cypress Vale. The overseer executed my orders. That was one fewer witness that I had to be concerned with, even if he was just an ignorant nigra.

All things went just as I had planned. All but one thing that I didn't foresee: Perry's wench, Cassie Mae. Somehow, Perry got hold of my note after the Yankees had read it. When he got to the plantation, he headed straight for Cassie Mae. Forrest reported that he shot Perry right in front of her. She fell on his body screaming and crying in hysteria. She must have taken the incriminating note off his person before Forrest's men could drag her away. Unlike her buck, that slave wench could read and write, an ability she owed to the kind heart, yet poor judgment, of your dear mother whose personal maid she had once been. She knew the value of the information that she had acquired and bided her time.

Grant took Vicksburg after a hellish siege. He paroled the Confederate soldiers who had formerly defended the city against him. Thus reprieved, I returned to the plantation to insure that things were running as smoothly as possible, for I knew that somehow we would rally and I would be re-assigned in the field. That is when Cassie Mae dared to try to blackmail me. What a bold nigra she was! In exchange for her silence, she wanted freedom for herself and her pickaninnies, _and_ she wanted land! I did not know what she had done with the note, nor did I know who else she might have told about it. She had an advantage, and she knew it.

I was furious. After tearing her cabin apart in search of the evidence against me, I found nothing. I wanted to kill her, but I did the next best thing. Some call it rape and assault; I call it putting a nigger bitch back in her place. She fought like a she-devil, but, of course, I won. Afterward, to keep her quiet, I gave her the scrap of land on the eastern outskirts of the plantation, where, unknown to her, I had instructed Forrest to dispose of Perry's body.

That aggravation paled in comparison to adding $100,000 in gold to the Pembroke fortune. Grant's siege had prevented my comrades from returning to Cypress Vale for the hidden treasure. Soon after Vicksburg fell into Union hands, I secured it in the mansion vault. Providentially, the men from my troop who had hidden it were all killed courageously defending Vicksburg when it was besieged. Thus, no military personnel remained who might accuse me of treachery or theft.

The money kept our family afloat during that damned
Yankee occupation of Mississippi and served as seed money to
to regrow our forturne.

I hope, now, that you understand, Adam. Being a man
requires many things; being a man of power demands
everything. After my death, you, my firstborn male child,
will be king and guardian of the Pembroke legacy. Rule well,
my son.

J. Pembroke
1875

Olivia had stopped several times in the course of her
reading. Only in segments could she process the lurid
account of all that Julius Pembroke had perpetrated,
otherwise her mind revolted against exposure to it.
When she finished, she was aware that one part of the
letter had impressed her mind more aggressively than
the rest and was demanding closer attention. She soon
realized that this was because it sounded so familiar.
It was Julius's concern about *his* legacy. Where had she
heard words like that before?

A sobering realization seemed to work its way
menacingly up her spinal cord and then grip her brain.
Nathan. She had heard such words from Nathan four
nights ago in her own kitchen. This acknowledgement
triggered a series of deductions: At the time of his death,
Perry and Cassia Marie had two children, both were
girls. Prior to that, Perry had been away with Julius in
his military service. He had not been with his wife for
possibly two years. Upon returning, he had barely had
time to greet her before he was murdered. Yet, later,
Cassie had borne a son, George Perry—after a violent

155

rape. The connection between the two acts hit Olivia like lead.

For some moments she simply starred at the letter, unable or unwilling to engage in further thought. Then rage began to ferment. Thoughts of lost honor, of wrecked family pride, of tainted lineage agitated it more and more until it erupted in an explosive shout, "NO!" Seconds later, ripped and torn fragments of yellowed paper littered the bedroom floor.

Wednesday
July 5, 2000
3:00 a.m.

The shrill ringing of the telephone on the bedside table sliced through her fitful sleep. Caller i.d. once again revealed the source of the call. She picked up the receiver.

"Hello?"

"Carlisle Forrest. That is the name that you wanted to know."

Olivia quickly sat upright amidst her tumbled linen. "Thank you. Thank you for doing the right thing."

"Blood ties *do* bind. . . .Olivia." There was a click and then the dial tone.

The next voice heard over her phone was that of the desk sergeant at the nearest precinct of the Vicksburg

Police Department. Recognizing her name, the officer quickly transferred her call to the precinct commander, who was very obliging. Ever since the shootings on Tuesday, arresting the person(s) responsible had been Priority #1 for Vicksburg's Finest. He assured her that a warrant would be issued and that the suspect would be apprehended within the hour.

After the call ended, Dr. Olivia Perry fell back onto her bed expecting to experience floods of sweet relief and, eventually, peaceful slumber. But neither came. Anxiety and a sense of impending danger stubbornly persisted.

"God, *something is still <u>not</u> right*! But *what*? Isn't all revealed now? Aren't the long-held family questions answered, Lord? Aren't the issues settled?"

She lay there in the darkness ... waiting, as she was accustomed to doing after crying out as she had. Waiting for an answer to be revealed to her intellect. "*... for blood it defileth the land: and the land cannot be cleansed of the blood that is shed therein, **but by the blood of him that shed it**.*"

"'But by the blood of him that shed it,'" she spoke the words out loud. Then, she started to apply the verse. "Perry's blood was shed and his body dumped on land that was later given to Cassie Mae, land that is now Nathan's. Julius Pembroke gave the order for Robert Forrest to kill Perry, so, though Forrest pulled the trigger, ultimately, Pembroke shed the blood. But how can either one of them pay for that crime with their blood? They've both been dead for at least a century. Wait a minute! Robert Forrest . . . Carlisle Forrest . . . Is there a connection? Yes! There must be. That's how the bloodline continues."

Then, her mind formed the subsequent conclusion: *"The bloodline of Julius Pembroke also continues on—in my son and in my grandson."*

The danger was not passed. An eminently greater force than Carlisle Forrest was at work in this, and *He* would use whomever He pleased to fulfill His word and His will. There was nothing more that Olivia could do. Self reliance was now bankrupt. She would simply have to trust God.

Wednesday
July 5, 2000
7:00 a.m.

"It's beautiful out here, especially at this time of day," Scott said in quiet awe. He seemed to be talking more to himself than to the person standing beside him. "God's morning glory is on everything." He then turned to the other individual. "What brings you here, Nathan? I was surprised to see your car drive up. At first I was afraid that something had gone wrong at the hospital."

"I,m sure that you were. It was a rough night. But I just wanted to see the property one more time while it's still mine. When I see it again, it'll be part of Apostles' Creed Christian Academy."

"Any regrets?"

158

"None. I've made my peace with all of that. Right now I just feel … free. And you're right; this is a lovely place. It's strange; now that I'm about to give it up, I feel able to fully appreciate its beauty.

"Are you still returning to Washington today?"

"No, John's son and daughter are flying in later this morning. You can imagine what they've been going through. Antoinette didn't want them to come until it was clear which way his condition would go. She said that she wanted to spare them the ordeal of waiting to see at the hospital. She's a strong lady."

"That she is," affirmed Scott.

"But even she has her limits. I'm going to stay to make sure that she, Meji, and Candace are comfortably accommodated while they wait for John to be transported to Washington. I'll probably be set to leave on Friday, and I'm going to try to convince Mother to fly back with us for a proper visit."

"Dr. Olivia Marguerite Chevalier Perry in the *political nerve center* of the nation?" Scott asked in surprise. "You like to live dangerously, don't you, Congressman?"

"Just intercede for us, Reverend," Nathan returned with a smile. "Oh, by the way," he added, "Cecilia's parents want to thank you for praying with her children on her behalf. They're sure that she'll want to thank you personally when she's stronger. She seems to have come through the worst of it."

"Thank God for that. When I left her situation was still pretty bad. I'm glad that she's pulled through."

"You obviously pray some powerful prayers, Reverend. And," he continued somewhat slyly, "you seem to have made a distinct impression ... . You *do* know that Cecilia is *single*, right?"

Scott looked at him in embarrassed exasperation but could not suppress a grin. "Man, don't start stuff."

"Okay, okay," Nathan laughingly relented. "I won't mess with you."

The minister prudently changed the subject at this point.
"You know, it really got to me to see John on that stretcher right after the shooting. He was lying there with his insides ripped up and bleeding; I could not believe my eyes. As a minister I know all too well that we are mere mortals, but somehow I've always thought of him as invincible," Scott admitted.

"You, too? I felt like so much of nothing when *I* saw him. Those bullets that he took, that *they* took, were meant for me. For *me*, Scott. I had guilt like you wouldn't believe. All I wanted to do was get to who was responsible, not just the shooters, but whoever sent them."

"I can feel what you're saying; I also wanted to pay back right then and there. But we would have been wrong to do that. That would have been revenge, not justice. Then we would have been intruding in an area that God reserves expressly for Himself," Scott cautioned.

"At the hospital, I was going to shut everything down right then and withdraw from the race. Then Antoinette said that John had asked her to give me a message before they wheeled him into the operating room."

"What was it?"

"Just two words: 'No fear,'" replied Nathan.

"That sounds like him. The police investigators said that he took out both of the snipers before he went down."

"Amazing. Yet and still, with the kind of injury that he sustained, he'll be laid up for a while. Maybe he'll take the time to do some soul searching. He needs to rethink a lot of things," Nathan observed thoughtfully.

"Yes, he does, and I pray that he will," Scott said earnestly.

"One thing still puzzles me. How did John get off the roof after he'd been shot? Nobody knew that he was up there, and he couldn't have made it down by himself in that condition."

Scott was silent for a moment. Then he said with certainty. "There's only one other man who could have known that he was there and who could have gotten him down before he bled to death."

Nathan looked at him and understood, but no name was spoken between them. *Both* of them would have to ponder for themselves the bond between John and this person who had put John's life at risk and then had risked his own to save it. But *one* of them would have to decide what the law would do about this comrade, this villain-hero whose name they silently agreed not to utter. Nathan mentally asked for divine guidance in that task.

Thus, the minister and the statesman conversed as they again stood at the fence between their separate properties, soon to become one. This time they stood on Nathan's side of the boundary. Again they in admiration surveyed the expanse of land. Perhaps if they had not been so engrossed, they would have noticed the "DEMETER" sign where there was the white glint of sunlight reflecting on metal.

The sharp crackling of rifle fire splintered the morning peace and Nathan Perry fell to the ground. Bright red blood splattered the grass, stained the dark earth.

Twice thwarted, Carlisle Forrest was now determined to achieve his objective.

"Nathan!" Scott exclaimed. He dropped down beside him and looked about them wildly, trying to find the source of the attack.

In his desperate flight, Forrest had managed to stay just one step ahead of the police, but even now sirens screamed in the distance.

"I'm okay," Nathan cried between clenched teeth. "I took it in the shoulder. Are you all right?"

"Yeah! Look, we've got to get off this open ground. If I help you up, do you think you could make it to the church?"

"I think so. Come on," Nathan said as Scott helped him to his feet, "let's move!" The two of them ran toward the sanctuary.

Instantly, another shot rang out, but from a different direction.

This time Carlisle Forrest fell dead with a bullet in his heart; his body collapsed across the sign. A crimson stream flowed from his chest, streaking across the name DEMETER and running onto the waiting ground.

The sign marked the place where, more than a century ago, the vast acres of Cypress Vale Plantation had yielded to the "scrap of land" and to the will of Cassia Marie Perry.

At the northern end of the Apostles' Creed property near the academic building, Jude Ramadan disassembled his weapon and quietly left the premises, seconds before police cars charged onto the parking lot.

(. . . "Vengeance is mine; I will repay." saith the Lord. – Romans 12:19)

The bones of Perry now rested in peace. His blood no longer cried out from the ground to be avenged. The land was purged of that innocent blood by the blood of *them* that shed it. But Nathan Sundiata Perry's life was spared, for far better Blood than his had redeemed it.

(Christ hath redeemed us from the curse of the law, being made a curse for us: for it is written," Cursed is every one that hangeth on a tree:" - Galatians 3:13)

The Curse Causeless | *Shall Not Come!*
|

|
|
|
|
|